Grace under Fire

*The Pursuit of
Restoration and
Refinement
in the Fires of Divorce*

Mackenzie Grace

ISBN 979-8-88540-326-9 (paperback)
ISBN 979-8-88540-327-6 (digital)

Christian Faith Publishing
832 Park Avenue
Meadville, PA 16335
www.christianfaithpublishing.com

Printed in the United States of America

Acknowledgments

To my parents

You have raised me to believe that even the furthest galaxy still isn't a limitation. You are my heroes. You've wept with me in my deepest pain, rejoiced with me in my every accomplishment, and grounded me in solid reality. You exemplify our heavenly Father with your unconditional love in the ways that you treat each other, those around you, and your children. And for that I am the woman that I am. I love you always, *Gracie.*

To my counselor Adele

You have seen my heart in the most vulnerable of places, spoken biblical truth to a wounded soul, and with grace continue to guide me to the places where healing, wholeness, and health are found. Thank you for doing the hard work, the Lord's work, and seeing me through both brokenness and binding.

To my tribe

To each of the women who have prayed over me when I couldn't pray for myself, to the sisters who fought in the battlefield of prayer as my battles raged around me, to the girls who held my hand in the fire and came out of the furnace next to me, to you I am thankful. Your presence in my life may have been quiet in the physical realm but never in the spiritual.

My heavenly Father

"In all my sorrows, Jesus is better." For this You made my heart truly believe. You have walked me through the darkest of valleys, and with me You have scaled the highest of mountains. You have never left my side. I find great solace in the truth that in all of life's disappointments—past, present, and future—You will never be one.

"Great is thy faithfulness."

Introduction

When the Walls Fall Down

*The Light shines in the darkness, and
the darkness has not overcome it.*

—John 1:5

Dear friend,

Is your life spiraling out of control? Do you feel it crumbling all around you? Are you shaken and worn out and beaten inside? Is the marriage you once believed in now broken and scattered in pieces like a broken puzzle on the floor all around you? Have you lost all sense of understanding and found it instead replaced by confusion and doubt and shame? Do you find yourself at a loss for words to explain your circumstances, yet aching for a comfort that soothes your weary soul? The harsh reality of divorce is so painful. Broken hearts prove to us that they are, in fact, both physical and spiritual. Our souls are weary and heavily burdened. I know.

Sister, if you would allow me, I want to be the one to speak some wholesome truth straight into your soul. To be the one to take your hand and remind you that there is still more to your story—this is only a chapter. And before you find me unintentionally reminding you of the pain you've lived or might still be living, I want to share my stories of hope with you.

I picture you on the other side of this saying, "Yes, yes! This!" Because the truth for me is when my world was upside down, I needed these reminders too.

This story is about so much more than the darkness and defeat and failure of a marriage lost. Rather, this is a story of hope and restoration and what that means for me and for you. It is written to shed some light into your darkest hours of pain because in the blurred lines that are confusion and betrayal, in the despair of the lonely nights, I want you to remember something profound. Dear girl, the most important thing that this all boils down to here is something that will mold you and shape you into a reflection of our Savior, something to remind you of the flourishing that will come with patience and pursuit, something that is good enough for all of mankind yet pursues you individually still. Remember these two simple words: God's grace.

Remember today that His plans are to prosper you, to never harm you. *Remember tomorrow* that His love is unconditional at worst when this worldly well of love runs dry, and *remember always* that *"he is fighting for you,* [because He wants to and] *you must only to be still" (Exodus 14:14).*

Don't quit. Don't you look around at the brokenness and the blurred lines and think for one millisecond that your life is over. That the life you thought you once had isn't worth living or breathing for or that maybe throwing in the towel is an acceptable choice. Don't think about walking away from Christ either, girlfriend, just because life didn't turn out the way we planned it. Nuh-uh. That's not how this faith business works. Let me be the one to break it to you. Though the winds are raging and the storms are fierce right now, though the walls are crumbling around you and the earth is shaking underneath your feet, though it feels like the sun has set and will never again rise over the disappointments and the setbacks of a broken heart and broken marriage, this is still *not* the end.

There is so much more waiting for you both within this trial and on the other side of it; so much working happening in your waiting; so much refining and grace and comfort to be found even within the darkest of moments; so much healing and wholeness to be completed for your bleeding and broken heart. All tailored to fit the size of your needs. Just around the corner of disaster awaits redemption that is chock-full of restoration. But only if you believe. And that is *exactly* how this faith business works.

When the most painful of trials awaits us, we must put on the armor that our God has ordained for us to wear. He has already provided us the necessary attire to weather the fiercest of storms. We must choose to equip ourselves with His protection: His Scriptures and our faith to see us through. No matter where you find yourself right here, right now, in this moment, I want you to recite John 1:5. Take a breath, lift your chin to the heavens, and declare that you, too, will see the light inside your darkness.

I say, "You too" because I have done it. I have lived it. You want the proof in the pudding? No problem; I got every flavor, lady, and I'm about to share it all with you. Speaking gospel truth is hands down one of the most combative moves you can make in this war. Checkmate. Do this as often as you can, as frequently as you can, hide it deep within the wounded caverns of your aching heart, and I promise you this—He will shine through to you. Every. Single. Time.

I trust that if you're reading this, chances are you've experienced this physically painful, emotionally challenging, and life-altering event. Maybe you're just standing there looking at these words, numb, knowing that you are all too soon heading into this deep, dark abyss and dare not even look to the day ahead. Or is it perhaps too late and you are inside already? Is it scary and lonely and you ache in pain from the deepest part of your being? I know, sister. I know.

Let me encourage you. Whether you're walking this dark and scary road, you know someone who is living the nightmare now, or perhaps you're counseling someone around you in this trial, my friend, *be still.* Take heart. Look around for God's presence. He is here, and He promises us this much—He isn't leaving. Deuteronomy 31:6 tells us, "*...He will never leave you nor forsake you.*"

Often divorce divides us unfairly. Sometimes we least expect it as a spouse announces their sudden departure. Unprepared much like death leaving us with more questions than answers. Frequently in our society, divorce has become a nonchalant agreement between two members of marriage resulting in the ultimate choice to take separate roads. Those instances often seem less tragic from the outside, but from any insider perspective, you might find these types are just as confusing and tumultuous to the human psyche and spirit as any unexpected ending to a sacred union. Perhaps you had no choice but to pull up your big-girl pants and run from an abusive marriage.

Whatever your source of divorce has been, it is nothing short of breathtaking. Fear lives and breathes within, friends. Confusion whispers into the depths of our being the second our souls find a quiet peace. But hold on just a second because I have a charge that I hope you will take as you lunge headfirst into the coming days, months, years, and the battles that await within them: the declaration to help you stand firm in the fire, dear ones. Strong in our ambition to fight the lies the devil has for us. Fight the lies that we are not good enough to overcome our pain because of our broken past. Defeat the shame and rip the scarlet letter from our shoulder declaring that we are unworthy of His love and acceptance. God is waiting for you to draw near to Him, daughter. And let me tell you about all the mercies He has waiting for you.

"The steadfast love of the Lord never ceases, his mercies never come to an end. They are new every morning. Great is your faithfulness" (Lamentations 3:22–23).

Within its realms you might feel the kind of pain that takes the wind out of your chest. Anxiety tags along and acts as a child of divorce. I've yet to meet a person who has avoided the side effects of anxiety even if they think they have. Much like a sudden storm, it tears your sails down and sets you sinking. Let me be very clear here as I describe the process. Divorce is a tactic from the evil one. It survives for the sole purpose to destroy you, destroy your family, your friendships, to destroy the union that God only intended for purity and unity, and holds the ability to take you far from grace if you allow it even the slightest of chances. Divorce is nothing short of brutal. Horrifying, atrocious, disgusting, shameful, tormenting, anguished, diseased—all of these words bear resemblance to monsters and are also too alive with their very presence. Words that carry more weight than most. Words that are sharp as a sword and have the ability to utterly destroy a human being's spirit.

Can you relate? Me too. Are you harboring some or maybe all of those disgusting words deep inside your heart and fearing of their truth? I can write this story to you because, friend, I know. I get it. I have felt it all from the breaking down of a sacred union to the weight of the shame as a divorced Christian. But hold on because as much as I have lived that life and all of those deafening words, I have also lived so much more.

And oh, my word, there is *so* much more. There is freedom. There is grace and joy and peace and to be found where the Spirit of the Lord is and all simply because our Savior desires these gifts for us. I have lived the broken road of divorce, but I have also found restoration of the most beautiful kind waiting for me in peace with Christ on the other side of it. And He wants all of this for you too. Please keep reading because I'm here to tell you something of utmost importance.

The same God who created the winds and the waves to obey His voice, the very same God who spoke this entire creation into existence in a mere seven days, He is walking along this dirty, splintered road right beside you. He knew all of this was going to happen long before we did. He hates that our hearts have been broken. But He still wants us to come running to His shadow.

"Those who live in the shelter of the Most High will find rest in the shadow of the Almighty" (Psalm 91:1 NLT).

I know what it feels like to harbor the loneliness of the pain, the shame of being a Christian woman walking a road that was *"never going to be me."* The fear of disappointing those closest to me both in family and even church, hiding from the gossip being whispered behind my back, the lies of the life I thought I once had. It's unfair. All of it. And exhausting. And tormenting.

But, sister, lean in close. Do I have your full attention yet? The truth is, even within all of the ugliness of divorce, even within that shame and guilt and disappointment, there is still a prolific beauty to be found within the ashes. And that beauty? Is that you are never too far from grace.

Often it feels like no one around you can truly understand your loss. Maybe they blame you. Often we are to blame. Often we aren't. But just trust me; when the days are dark, when the winds and the waters rage, I have found it imperative to my mental and spiritual health to have someone to be there for my accountability, for my growth, for my sanity. And if you would allow me the privilege of your friendship, that person could be me. Will you let me walk with you if only for a little while? Will you let me be the voice that reminds you just how loved you truly are?

If I was sitting with you right now, which is what I imagine as I sit in the quiet of the night in a messy living room and write these words to you, I would tell you of your worth to Jesus. I would tell you of the struggle He set within me and the disobedience that ensued before issuing this story to you. That the last thing in my heart was to publicize my pain and use it to set someone else free from their shame. You might call it a *limp in the blessing* kind of thing.

So let me say it all again while we're here soaking in our realities together. The very truth of the matter, the black and white of it all, the elementary of this world all falls on the same premise that you are loved. That the very same God who created the stars to sing and the rocks to cry out in praise created *you* for a purpose, dear girl. He created your inmost being and knew you even before this ugly, painful world did. He wants you to flourish in this lifetime. Of course He wants to use your talents and your gifts but *also* your pain and heartbreak to seek Him and glorify the kingdom and praise His name—to use the pain and fears of it all to draw nearer to Him no matter the circumstances.

Our struggles may seem overbearing to us. The culture may seem insensitive around us. Our church may not understand how it feels to be beaten with words or worse. But God does. I do.

That's why I'm writing this letter to you, friend. I'm writing to remind you that when it all feels like it's over, I can assure you, this is only the beginning of a new life, that even when you were hurt by the one person in this world you thought you could trust, even when you've been betrayed, deserted, abused, forsaken, or maybe, just maybe, you were the unfaithful one, there is still one man who calls you to His throne day after day; the very same one who calls you beloved. A man who will hold you fast and listen to your secrets without distrust. He will never let your soul be lost. A Father who will cherish your heart and restore your soul if you only ask this of Him. And a friend who will walk into those deep, dark, scary, hidden places with you and bring light unto your path.

Do you trust me to encourage you to help you seek Him? Do you trust Him to refine you and restore what has been lost? Come close. Listen, He's calling you by your name, daughter.

"And I will be a Father to you, and you will be my sons and daughters…says the Lord Almighty" (2 Corinthians 6:18).

1

Baby Steps

Women come to me after they hear my story. They want to share their stories of heartbreak too. Solidarity. I get it. I love it. Their glimpses of hope, their walks and processes of restoration—every, single one is just as important as the last. Never would I think that gratitude would be one of many emotions to follow me through my heartbreak and beyond; but oddly enough, it has.

Stranger things have happened. How wonderfully obvious it has become to me that this path of pain each of us are walking along may reach an intersection where we ought to experience an intercession of faith in our personal walks with each other. We meet somewhere along our trials and triumphs, with opportunity to share, encourage, weep, and rejoice together.

Thankfulness to God is necessary for me to express since my struggles have, at the very least, brought me this opportunity to minister to your weary heart, to love on you, to encourage you, sister, right here on the other side of this page. Thankfulness would be necessary if for no other reason than Jesus is on the throne. That we have a friend in the Creator and restoration on the other side of pain.

Thankfulness is much easier to talk about than to exercise. (Am I right?) How beautiful that our wounds can be used to show others the way to the cross. My heart is softened for you in your journey. My prayers are saturated with the desire that in all the disappointments you have faced, all the struggles this world has to offer, you

"

will choose to lean into Jesus and recognize that He truly is better than all of our sorrows. I'm reminded that in all of this life's utter failure and disappointments, He will never be one.

My thankfulness is that God brought these words to you in your season of brokenness and will use them to heal you, seek you, and draw you into deeper communion with him.

When I'm blessed with these opportunities to stop and chat with friends like you (and please, do stop and chat; I'm one of those never-met-a-stranger types), it's often the similarities that we've both been unlucky enough to experience that tend to catch my attention first.

Most of us have felt anguish in our humanity somewhere. If you're reading these words, I'm sure it's because you understand the pain. You know what it means to make every attempt to bury that hurt. To hush it just long enough to focus on our day-to-day lives. Do you go about your life hitting the snooze button (figuratively and literally), trying to catch a few more minutes to your dreams in order to avoid reality? Conversely, do you find yourself devoid of sleep, so you don't have to succumb to the quiet of the dark for fear of what awaits to haunt you in your dreams? Either way, we all have one thing in common. Eventually, we let that sneaky enemy into our minds just long enough to feed us the lies he wants us so desperately to hear: "I'm not good enough," "Life will never be better," "God would never want a sinner like me anyway." The truth is all of us experience the lies. Some of us are just better at hiding it.

Honestly, friend, I get tired of waiting. I'm depleted with waking up every day waiting for the validation in my ears. Wanting a human person to whisper truths to me. I want to hear that it's okay to be brave. That it's okay to be strong and that it's okay to be weak. That we don't have to live in this shame and those haunting lies. Hearing truth from wise people around us is necessary.

But one of the hardest lessons for us in the day and age where social media gives us shallow likes and loves is that *all of those phrases ironically mean nothing to my heart and soul if they aren't coming first from the one who created my heart and soul.*

I don't need that proof from anyone other than my heavenly Father. Our cups will eventually run dry without him. The truth is, He is saying all of that to you and me right now. He is always singing a love song to us. Listen. Do you hear the wind outside? Maybe the birds are chirping in a nearby park. Maybe children are laughing in a distant room.

God's creation is a love song written for you. Rain falls at His request, and snow is made silently, uniquely, at His demand. Just the same, He watches you every day as you struggle, as you smile. He writes a love letter to you every morning as the sun rises in the east and sings you a lullaby as the stars pulse in the quiet night sky. He constantly creates a space for communion with Him. Find yourself in a quiet moment, open your Bible, and read some of the grace He has written specifically for you. He took the time to write you a love story. Take the time to read it. I promise your heart will thank you for it later.

I believe this is our time. It's time that we step out of the darkness and fear of rejection and into the light of truth that instead tell us no matter our failures, our shame, our disappointments, no matter our heartbreak, our history, or the guilt of our past, we open our eyes to the realities that are waiting for us. On the *other* side of the lies, on the *other* side of the guilt and shame, the heartbreak and confusion, therein lies the simplest answer of hope our mere humanity could ever desire.

"And now o Lord, for what do I wait. My Hope is in you!" (Psalm 39:7).

So easily we forget the truth of hope. We forget the capability and access that we have to a world far greater than this one; the realization of the brokenness that we alone create attempts with ferocity to consume us. We have a Savior who is waiting for us. A mediator who wants to intervene into every corner of our brokenness and for us to only surrender our burdens that we may lay them down for Him to carry. A friend who is accepting our bitterness and reproach with open arms…

…And He is still calling us out. Calling us to wage war on the lies that are telling you to sit down and shut up. Wage holy hell on the fear

that sneaks around telling us that no one wants to hear what we have to say. Forward advance on the battlefield of faith and wreak havoc on the guilt that lies within FOR SUCH A TIME AS THIS.

We all fit in a category that could easily label each of us as *broken*. No one is exempt from the natural sin on this side of eternity nor the repercussions for it. Eventually after proper exposure and therapy, they begin the process of healing. Only over time do those wounds eventually turn into a scar. The thing with scars though is they still tend to hurt from time to time; often they never fully heal. Scars aren't always bad. They serve as a reminder of where we've been in this life. They tell a story. Sort of like a tattoo with the price tag of life. I hear you over there yelling at me, "Scars are ugly, ew!" Of course, they aren't pretty, girl. *Life isn't pretty.*

You can't always see people's scars. If you could see the heart, the wounds the battlefield of love has recorded, even the scars made from the Master Surgeon stitching it, mending it, molding it ever so gently back together, you wouldn't think it belonged in this small figure of mine. You might think it was the heart of a warrior. A warrior who has lived through much more than we ever truly give ourselves credit for.

But that's exactly what we are here. Those of us who carry the deep scars and somber wounds. The quiet ones who fight the good fight and continue, day in and day out, to carry our faith. We are the warriors. Sister, you are a warrior. But even warriors can be afraid to take that first step. And that's okay. What's important is that you never let fear win. Never let fear have the final say or any say. A very wise mentor of mine lives by this acronym of fear: false evidence appearing real. It's time to look fear in the face. Call it the liar that it is. And take that first, shaky (baby) step of *faith over fear.*

The armor of God is imperative to our walk on this earth for this very reason. In God's infinite design, He created an outfit for our combat. God gave us the spiritual outline of His armor for a reason.

War. You're in it. Whether you believe it or not, whether you see it or feel it or think I'm crazy, that's fine. War is raging all around us in the spiritual realm. Often, we ignore this truth because it makes us uncomfortable. Heck, it downright scares me to think there's an atmosphere of war happening around me, and I can't even see it. It's true though, all of it.

"For we do not wrestle against flesh and blood, against the rulers, against the authorities, against the cosmic powers over this present darkness, against the spiritual forces of evil in the heavenly places" (Ephesians 6:12).

Do you want to throw this book across the room yet? I know, right? Enough to scare the heebie-jeebies out of ya. *But wait! There's more.* Because Paul didn't leave us hanging out here in that world of fear. He continues in Ephesians with the steps to navigate our way through all this mayhem. Be sure every morning when you wake to put on the full armor of God. Verse 13 states, "Therefore, take up the whole armor of God that you may be able to withstand evil in the day, and having done all, to be able to stand firm."

Years ago, back in my college days, I had a great desire to write. I never had any promptings. I never felt that I had much to say or write about. Who would listen to a girl from the suburbs with a relatively quiet life? Not much to say…yet.

But a seed was being sown deep within my heart.

I had a professor of English who was a great encouragement to me. When my first college essay was nearly due, I recall working diligently in class. She came around to aid and assist in our work when she noticed my spacing on the computer was just a tad bit awkward (to say the least).

"What's going on here, Mackenzie?" She was so kind in her tone. I'm quite sure she offered some words of confidence before asking me that. "It looks like your paper has huge gaps between words here?"

I swear to you, as every homeschooler before me and every Generation Xer in 2005 who *had never owned a personal computer before now*, I looked right at her and said, "I'm sorry. I thought you said double space the paper. Did I do it wrong?"

Turns out? I had double-spaced *between the words.* (For anyone like me who's afraid to say they don't know, double-spacing is a cool little feature you toggle in your word documents that spaces out between lines. Not words. *Lines.*)

My spaces between words were big. So. Big. Like a-kinder-gartener-could've-used-my-paper-as-a-template-for-printing-and-learned-to-write-their-letters-in-those-spaces *big*. Like thick-as-you-wish-your-piece-of pie-at-Thanksgiving-to-be *big*.

Go ahead and laugh. I might've been homeschooled, but I somehow managed to graduate with honors and awards at the top of my college class, and I'm only telling you that just so you don't judge me (too hard anyway.)

Also, let that be the same lesson to you as it has been to me. Even when you don't know the very basics of something, God is still working it all out in the tiniest of details. After all, whose book are you reading? Don't let your fear stop you. If you're called to do it, do it. He will work it all out with faith and trembling.

The truth is, I never type a word or paragraph today without thinking about that poor teacher. If only she could see me now. But goodness, she was gracious, and I will love her forever for her quick and mild approach to fixing my *big* mistake. (Pun intended always.)

She didn't stop encouraging me either. Months later, she came to me with a paper I had written. Something unimportant, I'm sure. But in her words, she told me that she thought I had a gift for writing. That the way I wrote was engaging and impactful, and she hoped that one day I would pursue more writing. (That meant little to my immature twenty-year-old self.) I'm sure I thanked her, shrugged it off. But I never forgot her compliment. I hope she reads my words one day. And I hope she remembers that story about double-spacing and smiles.

Years later, many, many moons past my silly writing error in that musty basement college computer lab, I began to write again. Words started to flood my soul. I didn't really know where to take them, what to do with them, so I wrote them down on my computer in the late nights when kids were asleep, or in the daytime *only* after the house was clean, my then husband was at work, the kids were peaceful. After all, I had jobs to do. (And it was very clear to me that writing was not one of them.)

I shared a few *mom blogs* with my very best friends. One-page documents that outlined the struggles of life, without sharing too many of their gory details, for the simple fear of someone else realizing the truth I was living with. Some of them were funny. Some of them were sad. Most of them were encouraging. Looking back, I think I was trying to encourage myself to stay strong in the fight for my life. Literally.

Months later, after my separation from my husband, those documents were discovered on our shared computer. I had secretly hoped he would open them, find some promise in my work. Remind me (and him) that I am still a person with dreams and that I should consider pursuing writing more often.

But instead, he didn't encourage me. He didn't read them and recognize my love for reading literature had turned to a dream of writing literature. Instead, he scolded me for finding the time to write them when I should have been working. He reprimanded me for thinking my words were of any value and hushed the woman inside of me screaming to have her own voice. The same woman who writes to you right now. Same, but *very* different.

I obviously didn't recognize at the time how impactful that was to me. Honestly, my mind was already bruised, my spirited crushed, my heart broken from the harshness laid upon me. That's all I really want to share about that pain. Because my story, this story, isn't about being broken but rather finding the beauty within the brokenness.

It's taken me a few years to put *pen to paper* again and share this story of restoration with you. That would be because it *takes a few years* to experience restoration, and refining isn't something that happens overnight. What I didn't realize in my sadness for all of that was that my dream of writing had already been seeded deep within me. It wasn't stagnant. It was simply trying to push through the soil and bloom wildly. And that's the hardest part. *Pushing through the pain.* I had some anger to work through and doubt reminding me that he always said my writing "wasn't enough." And then one day, God whispered to me, *"I AM enough. Write for me."*

Even when I was being told "I can't" or "I have no business writing" or my "stupid mom blogs" were pointless, they weren't. God was using that pain to open me up. He was taking that knife being twisted in my heart and that lump in my throat and *culturing it to create* more.

As the vulnerability of having my words verbally shredded in front of me by the one human I wished would enjoy them the most, I noticed something. Just because he said no doesn't mean God did. My heart physically aches when I remember that pain. How badly I wanted his approval of my few words and the validation from the man that I had loved, just to encourage me. Just to be proud of me. That hurt me the most. But when I reconsider all of that, oh how it must have hurt God that His validation wasn't the first approval I should have been seeking all along.

Those words in those blogs weren't meant for anyone else. Those first few pages of documents were meant for me. They were a chance to catch a glimpse at the woman within, the woman God created, the woman I could be if *only* I believed in her. But these words, these pages, these documents, they were meant for you.

It's up to me now. God has given me the tools. The kind that heals, the kind that grows, the kind that encourages others around me. The armor to wage through the wars and the scars to prove His miraculous healing powers. He's given me the words to speak truth to you. It's time to put fear in the back seat, to remind him who's in the driver's seat, and to shut the lies off. Don't let anyone tell you that you aren't valuable. That the gifts God has given you aren't real or worth something priceless. That whether they are being a stay-at-home mom, a working mom, a single woman, a woman trying to navigate her way through this scary world like the rest of us, God says you are valuable in His sight.

You are precious in His eyes. You are more than enough to Him even with all of your bumps and bruises. Bring your gifts to Him, the tools He has buried within your heart, and let's use them together to cultivate a generation of strong women who are building up the kingdom together. It takes courage to push through the pain. It takes bravery to embrace what might be if we just step out in faith and use our gifts for grace.

Pursue. You never know what great plans God might have for your talents if you don't utilize them. And there's little time to waste.

Persevere. Declare grace within your words and actions. When you are meeting with the person who hurt you the most in your life, remember that he, too, was created in God's image.

Progress. When you talk about the lies spoken to you or the vulgarities you answered to, remember that *"soft answers turn away wrath" (Proverbs 15:1)*.

Baby steps.

God honors each and every step we take closer to Him. He sees you. His arms are open. And He's waiting for you to draw nearer to Him. Will you let Him mend your broken heart? Will you let Him use your scars for His eternal glory? It's time to take the first step. *Forward march.*

2

Strength in Pain

I am so weak. Basically, I can't open a dagum jar of pickles by myself or tighten a screw to save my own life. But that's a story for another day. Weak spiritually. Mentally too. Have you ever felt weak on a level that left you exhausted? Weak even to a point where maybe you can't imagine waking up and doing all of *this* yet again for one more day? I think it's fair to say that most women, even if we choose not to admit it, have without a doubt experienced this frailty. The trouble isn't in the *feelings* though. (Not always anyway.) The problem instead lies when we choose to ignore it, hush it, even cover it up for the sake of *having it all together*.

You know what I mean. "I'm fine!" Share a smile, maybe a hug, laugh about something the kids did this morning or the normal stressors of life before we walk away alone and remember *we aren't really fine*. Are you with me yet? If we want to combat this weakness that we know deep down we all have, we need to be vulnerable enough about it and be able stand up for the truth. We need to acknowledge that this is a real problem; that there is nothing wrong with not being fine and finding enough strength to ask for help. How else do we expect to mature in life and grow ourselves?

The fact of the matter is, I'm not strong enough to handle any of this myself. I wasn't created to do any of this by myself either. The divorce, single mothering, working, churching, volunteering. My best friend with three kids isn't strong enough to raise or discipline them without a little aiding and abetting from her husband and family. Raising tiny disciples is no joke!

They will bend you until you break. *(Ask me how I know.)* My missionary cousin isn't able to bear the load of a broken and suffering world in Haiti all on her own accord without the benefit of wise counsel. The pain would consume her. It dang near tried. But grace. Even my therapist isn't strong enough to manage all the emotional baggage I unload on her by herself. That's a tough calling. Listening to other people and their broken lives all day, teaching us to compartmentalize, and then turning the lock and doing the same for herself? I assume her mansion in heaven will be the talk of the town as it dang near should be.

The fact of the matter is the sooner we recognize that we—*none of us*—are in position to handle this world on our own, the better off we become. Community is what we were created for. And that's what I hope to create here for us. A gathering of wounded women, some burned, some burned out, all aching but also seeking the kingdom, and together we can use our pain to bring each other closer to Christ and use our brokenness to further the kingdom, all with the common goal of bringing Him glory through our restoration process.

The first pretty basic lesson I want to share with you, if having learned anything throughout my road to divorce, is that Christ is not going to leave me or you right here in the midst of our pain. He doesn't expect us to be strong on our own and to wake up and just handle the anguish that is a broken heart, a broken spirit, and a broken home all on our own. I'm reminded of 2 Corinthians 12:9, which states, *"But he said to me, 'My grace is sufficient for you, for my power is made perfect in weakness. Therefore I will boast all the more gladly about my weakness, so that Christ's power may rest on me.'"*

Let me make something clear here. Friend, I am not writing any of this to boast about my shortcomings and how God endowed them. Writing this seemed like a complete and utter nightmare to me if I'm speaking truthfully. The last thing I wanted to do fresh off of a painful divorce was open myself to more vulnerability and exposure to possible criticism while still in the healing process myself. I am writing this to you because, well, as crazy as this sounds written down on paper, God told me to do this. Crazy. Told ya.

As I sat down to pour my thoughts out, my plans were to speak words of affirmation to my sisters in Christ, mostly how we ought to rely on God, how we ought to seek after Him in the dark (anything but divorce). Even writing about the struggles of being a single mom seemed a *much* easier assignment to accomplish than writing about the very thing that shook me to my core. Divorce.

But you see, in the beginning, I wasn't doing what God told me to do. Nearly six months passed before I willingly obeyed God's calling to write these words to you. From my perspective, writing about divorce is scary, but living out a divorce is an all-out nightmare. Instead, I had some conversations with God about it all. We have lots of those, me and God. Conversations. This time, they went something like this:

"Okay, Lord, I feel you. I know You've given me this desire and urge to write. I can barely ignore it anymore. You've proven to me that other people want to read what I've written. You've approved the publishing of my other articles when I assumed that would never happen. I know You're giving me the nudge to walk this road. Now, let me just write about…x, y, z, and we'll see what happens. Cool? K. Good talk."

I would sit down in the evenings over the next few months and begin to take notes. Some short stories were made from it, nothing more, nothing less. Delete.

I found myself a few months later in the exact same position (physically and spiritually) on my couch, asking of God, *"Okay, here we go again. This time, give me the words to write encouragement to your children. Words of affirmation to addicts and abusers and broken people, words that will lift them closer to You. And maybe give me a name in the writing world."*

Can you see my spoiled, rotten honesty here? Can you guess what happened? Or rather, *didn't* happen. Words. They didn't come. Go figure. I spent more nights cutting and erasing word docs than I even care to admit.

But then something with a little more weight happened. God didn't give up on me just yet. That's just so like grace, ya know? Still showing up when nothing ought to be fair. Nothing owed to us. Still giving us chances when we really don't deserve them. I felt that same, almost annoying tug at my heart. That same anguish rolled around inside, and all I could imagine was another woman—like you—in her pain, sitting around alone at night like me. Wondering if anyone else felt the same way as her. Scared and alone. Trying so hard to navigate through her weakness and pain yet knowing somehow that God is still good. Though afraid of what the new and unknown future might look like. Needing a friend to remind her that in the end, it all really does work out; the war has, after all, already been won.

God told me right then and there I can be that friend. I've read the whole book. Cover to cover. Turns out, sister, we really do win! I have walked this road. I have allowed God to work within me. I have had women speak truths into my life with the benefit of growing closer to Him. And now, it's my turn.

Third times a charm they say, right? But this time was going to be different. I just knew it. But it

wasn't without a little humbling first. *"Okay, Lord. I'm here for this. All of me this time. Please, forgive me for my desire to control. Grant me the grace and the words that only You know women need in their broken roads of divorce. Let me be your voice of love to them and guide them closer to You both in my words, actions, and testimony. Here I am God. Go ahead and use me."*

And you know what happened next? Words. These words. They flowed onto the computer screen sometimes faster than I could even type. Memories of how Christ brought me through the fire and refined my heart shone like a projector in my head. I would stay up half the night feeling like the fire burned in my soul. It all began to make so much more sense now. The puzzle pieces finally fitting together in my story—the road I had walked, much like yours, full of heartbreak and uncertainty, was riddled with goodness and faithfulness for this very moment. For these words. For me and for you.

When you lay it all down on paper, the black and white, the good, bad, and the ugly, there was a solid reason that I was told to complete this task. It's been the most vulnerable part of my existence. The hardest task I have ever completed. To write about my wounds, laying it all on the line, knowing that some will scoff, all the while praying that others won't. But if God has proven one thing to me in the last few years of my life, it's in the simplicity that I *can* trust Him entirely, and that I *should* trust Him entirely.

Someone once told me that my writing years ago was a form of therapy. I believed that. So much so that I continued to do it and well, look where we are now. I also wholly believe you should be journaling your thoughts, especially in the *fire*. Your happy thoughts and your sad thoughts deserve to be written down. It will help you distinguish your thoughts from reality. Writing provides clarity for the situation and is concrete. The beautiful thing is, you can literally put this chapter of your life on a shelf or in a box in the attic or in a bonfire if you wish (I won't tell) and move on with your life. It will help, I promise you.

But there's more to this chapter. You see, I didn't write all of these words just to tell my story. There was a reason for all of the experiences and the pain that I have lived, and I fully believe in the grand scheme of life that reason was you, sister. That wherever you are finding these words, whether by a lamp in a quiet room, maybe a little corner of your favorite coffee shop, or a few stolen moments on a lunch break, that you are reading these words for a reason.

Understand something of utmost importance here. *You* are worth these words and worth the discomfort that it takes for me to face my demons because God believes that you are worth seeking out. And I believe that you and I can use our broken hearts and broken stories together in order to love Him even more, to glorify His kingdom, and to reach the hurting world around us.

How desperately I needed (and still need!) friends to speak truths into my life and to walk along this treacherous road with me. I needed to be built up and encouraged and reminded that God wants to take my ashes and turn them into something beautiful. He wants to do this for you too. He wants to take every shattered piece of your broken heart that is scattered in fragmentations around your living room floor and bind them up into a new creation. Psalm 34:18 (ESV) tells us, *"The Lord is near to the brokenhearted and saves the crushed in spirit."*

He desires to see you whole again and at peace. He wants you to be *free indeed* from the aches that torment your being and the sorrow that consumes your soul. The beautiful thing about all of this though is that He wants you just the way you are. Right now. In this moment. And He loves you for all of it.

But none of this comes for free, friend. You see, He won't do any of these good things without

us. The truth is, God absolutely makes things new when we seek that from Him. He can take your ashes and mold it and form it into something more beautiful than you and I can ever imagine. Reality check! He did create the entire universe in less than seven days. *Obviously,* He's highly qualified for the job position. My point here is this—He *can* fix our brokenness. But He certainly doesn't have to. This is where we come into play.

When I sit down with friends who are struggling in their marriages, these are the truths that we

discuss firstly. Remember, I believe that giving you these promptings in this season of your life is acceptable for the simple reason that I myself have lived it. I have been served papers. I have walked the steps into the courthouse, and I have experienced both the shattered brokenness and the binding of my heart by Christ our Savior. I am a mere human, far from any resemblance of perfection; but within the process, I have experienced refining and learned how to draw closer to Christ than even I knew possible by following the guidelines given to me by wise counsel and devout, beautiful-hearted

Christian women who have loved me even at my worst. I want the same for you. And so does Jesus.

I cannot stress enough to you how imperative is the choice that we ought to be seeking Christ

in our lives with every facet imaginable.

Seeking out Bible studies where other women will be holding you accountable for your investment in the truth. *Serving* in some capacity within your church walls where you are surrounding yourself with like-minded people who will pour grace and love back into you.

Getting on your face when the future is uncertain and *lamenting* in tears to God over the brokenness of your heart and spirit and the anguish that torments your every thought.

We ought to be living out His words for our lives and walking in the truths that He has waiting for us. We absolutely have to lay down our pain and our baggage and our confusion and our doubt and our fear and say, *"Hear I am, God! All of me! Every broken fragment, every anguished piece of my heavy heart. Go ahead. Go ahead and try."* And then, sister, then?

…Faith.

Are you weak like me? Are you hurting and lonely and afraid? He doesn't tell us to be strong on our own. Quite the opposite, really. He tells us to be weak. That it's okay to be fragile. Otherwise, His power would have no place in our lives. If we could do it all ourselves, if we were made to handle all the trials and brokenness on our own accord, we would have no need for the power and perfection that we find in Christ alone. Give your weakness and doubt and fear to God and let Him use these traits to show His strength in your circumstances.

More than once during my divorce, friends would tell me it seemed I was being so strong. *"How are you doing so well?"* They would ask, *"How are you keeping it together?"*

I laugh when I think of these comments. (Girl, you shoulda seen me crying a river in my car an hour ago.) Begging God like Jesus both before my marital separation and after to *"take this cup from me? Don't make me walk this road. Don't allow it!"*

The only real answer I have for keeping my act together was this simplistic knowledge that will no doubt enable you to get through the pain: I am weak, but He is strong.

To this very day, I still find rest in that knowledge. Of all the things I absolutely have to be—mom, employee, housekeeper, chauffeur, volunteer—I don't have to be strong on my own. There was nothing I could do to fix my circumstances. But God could. He didn't give me my husband back. He didn't fix all of my earthly problems. But He did do a lot of other things. He walked through the fire with me. He made sure I was not burned up in that furnace, and

He walked out of that tribulation holding my hand. I chose to praise Him in the storm. And, friend, it's your turn to make the choice too. This, right here, is the reason I'm writing this. And I believe it's the reason you're reading these words.

In the last few years of life, I've witnessed more than one friend go through trials and choose to walk away from God. My heart hurts especially when I see how lost they are out in this big, crazy world. Don't let the temptations of this world suck you in.

It's so easy to drink a little extra wine to feel happy again, but it won't last for more than a few hours or a night before it consumes you instead of you consuming it. Be filled with the Spirit of the Lord and lean into him in the darkness.

Spending extra hours on social media to avoid the painful reality is too easy today, and I promise it will leave you lonelier with comparison than when you first began. Try fasting from some apps for a while. Your heart will find peace almost instantly.

Working out physically also allows room for mental health but in excess can be unhealthy if it takes the place of spiritual growth. All of these vices will only lead to comparison, and comparison is the thief of joy.

Remember this instead. *"The Joy of the Lord is my strength."* True joy can only come from one place and that is the Father. When we come to Him first, when we cry out with every single burst of hurt, anguish, fear, anxiety, uncertainty, defeat, He will meet you right where you are. Waiting with His arms open full of grace and peace and love and sharing all of it with you, dear girl. The beautiful thing about it all is, He will be the first one to understand it all, because don't forget, He once lived on this forsaken earth too.

This is just the beginning of a very long war, sister. I know it hurts to read those words. It's enough to traumatize you without ever entering the trivial court process. But until you recognize the very real battle for your soul that is happening all around you, you won't be able to fight properly.

"For we do not wrestle against flesh and blood, but against the rulers, against the authorities, against the cosmic powers over this pres-

ent darkness, against the spiritual forces of evil in the heavenly places" (Ephesians 6:12).

The battles during divorce are enough to deplete you of joy; don't allow it. Remember the truth instead; when you are walking into the scariest places, when it feels like the world is crumbling around you, "He will never leave you nor forsake you."

The battle for your soul is also raging. The choice is yours now. Will you choose to take His hand and let Him guide you through this? Will you choose to give God the glory and be still in the wait? Proverbs 31:17 reminds us of the godly woman. *"She girds herself with strength."* I don't know about you, but I aspire to be her. I can't gird myself with my own strength, but I can clothe myself with the strength of our mighty Lord. And who wouldn't want that?

Lean on the Father. Make a conscious choice every morning and every night to choose Him. Ask Him to help you get through the confusion, the doubt, the physical and spiritual trials with grace. And, dear sister, put on your armor. The battle awaits. Just don't you forget something in the middle of this battle—the war has already been won.

3

He's Working in the Waiting

I had a dream one night recently. Like most nights, I put my girls to bed and tidied up our little home. Being a single mom is no joke. There are a thousand words to describe it, but living it leaves you basically speechless when you attempt to verbalize the task. Overwhelming seems best. It's easy to stay busiest during the day. There's just so much on our plates, the hardest job being the tendering and guiding of the little disciples we call children. We are, after all, the first ambassadors of Christ that our children will know.

But if you're like me in any way, it's immensely painful to look around and see what appears to be happy families surrounding you. At school, at church, at the beach, at the grocery store. Sometimes our eyes lie to us though, don't they? We only see what we want to see or what the devil wants us to see. I used to be one of those families that appeared to have it all together. Smiling on the outside, aching on the inside. Waiting for the tide to change from constant pain to cheerful relief. The reality is, there's so much hurting all around us, we're often blind to the pain of others too. The pain that nearly half of us are living with and hiding deep down inside (or within the four walls of our homes.)

For me, it's easy to feel the loneliest at night—at home—in the quiet. Is it the same for you? When the laundry is washing and the dishes are piled in the sink, homework papers needing attention, bills overdue and hidden from sight, lunches needing packed and crying children waking in the night for drinks or potty breaks or fevers. Sometimes I just wish someone, anyone, would say, "I got this tonight, babe. Rest." And honestly, I still wish for this more often than I probably should.

This particular night of my dream, though, like any other night, I emptied the dishwasher and switched a load of laundry. Packed some lunches for school for my girls. Probably cried a few self-loathing tears before I dragged my exhausted self into a quick shower. But God always knows, doesn't He? When we feel the loneliest, that's really just our humanity sneaking in and reminding our sick hearts to be stubborn and selfish. As Christians, we probably ought to know better. We know we're never *really* alone. I could've chosen to read my Bible and listen to the truth. I could've found some solace in some worship music or even called up a girlfriend, but no. Not this night. Instead, I chose the quiet and pity of my own deceitful heart. *Bad life choice.*

Now, I've heard people discuss about how God speaks to them. Whether by prophecy, audibly, maybe visual, it's always mysterious. It's really quite fascinating when you consider the ways God engages with His children. He speaks to me in many ways. Often it sounds like this though: "*I told you so.*"

Other times it's in dreams. Often, I have a vision in my heart that I wake in the early morning hours to. No matter how, I'm sure it's the work of the Holy Spirit simply because it's never an image that I would create on my own. Most of my friends would tell you I'm not a very creative person. Crafty yes. Creative without Pinterest? Absolutely no. Art does not come easily to me. Just ask my college art professor. (I earned that hard C in elementary art education.)

This image often given to me within the night, it always pertains or relates to something weighing heavily on me. Something that I haven't even uttered a word about yet to my dearest friends. It's always understood. Like someone looked deep inside and felt my pain or struggle in that moment, created a piece of artwork, and then stuck it on the fridge inside my brain. It's like He gets me every single time. Because He does.

This night as I was burdened with my brokenness, I saw the image of a heart. Not a silly valentine's heart but a rather textured image; kind of gruesome. I don't like gruesome. This heart had scars and veins and wounds pulsing over it. It had stripes burned into it that appeared to be white with infection. Sick.

That's not all I witnessed. In the background, blurred in vignette, two hands held this heart. In those hands was a beige-colored string. Thick like twine. The twine was slowly stitching together the gaping cuts on the heart. It didn't appear that all the wounds were healed. Nor did it appear that the hands were furiously working to stitch the wounds with any haste. *("Be still, child.")* Typical. One more thing that wasn't going my way. Just a broken heart that wasn't healing quick enough. That was it. That was my dream. Pretty boring, right?

As the days went by, I considered this vision, or whatever you want to call it. What could it possibly mean? Why does everything have to be so mysterious with God? Is there more to this vision? It's so like me to want to fix my problems right now. (Impatience is a strong suit of mine.) Waiting on someone else, anyone else, makes me anxious. Waiting for kids? Exhausting. Waiting on hold? Torture. Lines at the car wash? Rolling my eyes so hard right now.

After a few days of lingering over the image of this broken heart, gruesome in all its intricate details, it took me a while to recognize. That was so like God. You see, God isn't on my time frame. He isn't sitting on His throne checking his Apple watch declaring that my problems and my overwhelming schedule and my court dates and my broken heart are going to magically be solved, completed, and healed in weeks, months, or even years. Or ever actually. Yet His promises still remain. *His promises are timeless.* They don't come with a prenuptial agreement and a warrantee for when conditional love runs out. Remember something with me, sister? *His power is made perfect in my weakness.*

Every once in a while, that same dream pops into my sleep. I never know when it will come. It never seems to be on any particular day or after certain events. But it is constantly changing, that heart. Some days the gaping wounds have been sewn and healed; fewer strands of twine appear. What's left behind, though, are the scars.

This heart looks healthier; no more infection, less blood and open wounds. I suppose that's life though. Fragile. My heart has a story to tell. And someday, yours will too.

Listen in the quiet for God. He's working. When you're giving Him your wounded heart, He's holding it. Stitching it ever so slowly back together. Making a masterpiece for His glory. We just don't always get to see the progress, but someday, oh someday, I hope we get to see the end result.

4

Destruction

Just when I think I'm doing fine, as I'm getting myself back to a normal routine where I'm on track to being physically, mentally, and emotionally well, that's when it creeps it. That's when doubt likes to jump right back into the little crevices created by my wounds and ask me a bunch of nonsense questions. Seriously, anxiety. *Can we not?*

My anxiety sets right back into full swinging motion. You know those cool rides at amusement parks and state fairs? The ones that buckle you in with a lap belt of steel and then throw you around for a few crazy loops? Just when you think it's done and it's slowing down (much like my life), it begins twirling in a different direction, sometimes backward, and swivels and swirls and twists some more. I feel like that's a pretty accurate—albeit fair—description of anxiety.

I mean, I'm human. You're human. Even God was in human form for a little while. And the fact of the matter is, we can't escape the probability of these sufferings that betray us. There is one thing I *am* sure of though. One solid reminder that never fails me—confusion is certainly *not* of the Lord. (Frankly my sweet, sweet counselor has to be *so* tired of repeating this to me because *honestly*, I get tired of repeating it to myself.) It amazes me how when I often feel I'm at my spiritual peak, that's the ample time zone when I have a large red target on my back. The devil must sit off on the sidelines, masquerading like an occupied spectator. Really, he's the matador running around with a brilliant red robe swaying in the wind, "Over here! Come get me! I'm ripe for the pickin'!"

My friend, there is good news to be found even though that does happen. And even way on the other side of this thing still happens, when the doubts, questions, and fears of reality also seem to be at a record high, the good (actually *great*) news, though? Is that it doesn't have to last. Those lingering fears and turmoil that attack your emotions and thoughts like parasites will only live on as much as you let them. *They only grow with the right ingredients; the trick is, don't water them! Don't feed them and harvest them! Don't give growth to a weed, and it won't fester into a forest.*

When all of this happens to me, I engage with the Lord. I sit down with his Words and remind myself of the black, white, and red truth. The Bible is readily available to you today. There's no excuse for not diving into it with every doubt and attack that comes at you.

So what exactly *does* God say about deceit? (Since deceit is a form of confusion, we can be sure to combat both by scripture and knowledge.)

"The heart is deceitful above all else" (Jeremiah 17:9).

Ouch. Wish I would have taken that more seriously ten years ago. (Insert hard roll of my eyes and a show of hands. Anyone else?) That's the paradox with love and divorce. Maybe your situation was much like mine. You can still have all the expectations, all the love for your spouse, all of the *feelings* and emotions and desire, but for many of us, you know that *feelings* can be highly toxic or inappropriate to human choices and that includes when they show up in the process of divorce and healing.

Feelings cannot be the judgment of what is pure and true and healthy and holy.

It doesn't seem very fair that love can be so double-minded, does it?

"But grace, o beautiful grace. Making sure life's not fair" (see: Relient K).

My kids like to play this game in the car. Honestly, it makes me a little bit of a crazy person, but their giggles implode from the back seat without a doubt every time. *"What if…*a unicorn came into our house and ate our food and…" "*What if*…we rode on the clouds and a giant alligator came swimming over…" Do you get the gist? This, my friends, goes on for as long as I allow it. I try to calm them down before someone inevitably giggles a little too much and causes a bit of a bathroom conundrum, but alas. Kids.

Aren't we so guilty of the same exact thing though? Have you experienced the confusion yet? The what-if questions? The days where you can hardly focus on "*What if I change myself? Maybe he'll love me more. What if I work more hours and get a new job? Maybe he'll see that I can 'pull my own weight.' Maybe I can just be smarter, prettier, funnier, and say I'm sorry so many times…what if?*"

I can assure you that if your answer was a resounding no and you have yet to fall into the pit of confusion, trust me, it will come in like roaring waves and roll out like a rising tide taking all your sanity right along with it.

Often the questions come like a hurricane destroying our days with cluttered mind and flooding our weeks with memories (both good and bad) when we allow them. It makes it nearly impossible to be focused and driven. The doubts crawl into the quiet stillness when we think we aren't noticing.

Often the confusion would find its way into my mind when I would be driving alone for work. The questions would cause me to wonder, *Did I do everything I could? Why couldn't I do enough or be enough for him? How come he doesn't love me enough to see how much he's hurting me? Why couldn't I have a better job / better income? How come I can't make him happy? Why am I such a failure? What can I do to make him see me?*

And later, the same questions came to play. It was when I knew, with fact and no longer speculation thanks to my close girlfriends and social media dating sites, that he was moving on from our marriage and into other relationships. Now, friend, I personally never struggled with the idea that I could go back to what once was. I knew my marriage was over long before I ever wanted to admit that it was. But that doesn't mean that it didn't sting a little inside seeing his dating profile for the first time. That thing that was *never* supposed to exist. That feeling struck me a little inside knowing that was supposed to be us—forever. That's when the questions creep in. The *what-if-I-asked-him-to-try-again* questions.

This is a dangerous cliff to be on, sister. And if this is you right now, let me just start by saying *there is no shame in the lonely.* In fact, I guarantee you without repentance that every *single* person you meet would tell you that at some point or another they, too, are lonely. This is normal. But please, do not choose to seek out what *once was* for the panic and momentary fulfillment of a lonely season.

There is a lonely like no other when you are divorced. It does not measure up to or even compete with the solitude of being single before marriage. The difference being having once maintained a relationship and union with someone who was at once our best friend and now is no longer, and at worst now an enemy, leaves an emptiness deep inside our being. A longing for what we know is emotionally and physically possible and tangible.

Reality check: raw emotions cannot be and will never be the authority of healthy choices.

Feelings cannot come before faith. Stand firm where you are. Seek out the Lord in the dark hours of the evening. Invite a girlfriend over to watch a movie, listen to some encouraging podcasts, open the Scriptures, and read out loud! But whatever you do, do *not* seek out what was once your marriage or any other physical or emotional relationships (and the benefits that ought to come in the sanctity of marriage) in order to cope with the sadness and the loneliness of a broken heart. They will leave you more destitute than when you began this journey.

Get your highlighter ready and mark this page so you can remember this when the desire for companionship becomes overwhelming. It's going to happen. Maybe not today, maybe not the day that you swore off ever getting married again. (Yep, I said that too.) Maybe not the day you swore no man would ever betray you again and you would rather be single and alone forever (been there). Maybe not the day you look up to the heavens and ask God, *"Aren't you ready to come back yet?"* (Totally might've done this too.) But you will feel lonely. You know how I know?

1. I've lived this road you're walking. I've drawn so close to God that I've cried out in grief for my ex-husband's forgiveness/grace/protection/mercy.
2. Jesus lived it. There is not one emotion ingrained in our beings that Jesus did not suffer at the hands of His accusers and murderers. He has felt abandoned and betrayed by His best friends. He has loved his neighbors and watched them line the streets as they spat on Him. He healed bodies and raised people from the dead, and we turned around and killed Him. If anyone has felt lonely? It would be our Messiah hanging on that cross alone, naked, torn to pieces, unrecognizable as the very Creator Himself turned and looked away.

"Eli, Eli, lama sabachthani?" [translated: "My God My God! Why have You forsaken Me!"] *(Matthew 27:46 KJV).*

Don't you think that God understands the loneliness? Don't you think for one split second that He knows better than any of us how it feels to be broken, betrayed, and alone? Jesus experienced all of this on this earth. His *best friend* betrayed Him. We betrayed Him. But here's the paradigm of the whole thing. The really good stuff that you can't get to until you've suffered a little while: There's grit to be found within the grace.

He *wants* us to crave relationship. He created you to want companionship. When He knit you together in your mother's womb, *He put that desire in you.* He could actually give you everything you're looking for and more. Come to him. *"All who are weary and heavy burdened, and he will give you rest…" (Matthew 11:28).*

Break down. Be lonely. It's okay. Bring it all to your Maker and tell Him about the struggle of the quiet nights, the days where the phone doesn't ring once, the desire for a man's touch or a simple spin on a dance floor. *The desire to be desired.* Tell Him. He's listening. But leave it at His feet and rest. Because He wants you to seek Him and be fulfilled in Him *first*. Do that. Choose Christ first. Focus your faith and fears on Him—and fully surrender to Him in every detail of this divorce. He will help you and aid you in your ability to get through the loneliness. Wise choices. *Because regret is real.*

But there's something else I want you to remember. And that is that we also serve a God who not only is in the business of making something out of ashes, He delights in it. Don't forget that nothing is a lost cause in the Potter's hands, and we are His clay.

He is not in the business of wasting things.

These are the moments though. The tough ones where we can choose to go astray, listen to the what-if questions. Revel in them and try to do things on our own. Why do those questions earn a place in your heart and mind, my friend? The truth is that they haven't paid for residency. Toss up that no-vacancy sign and remind them of who is in charge of those thoughts creeping in. You and God.

What if you found some hope for healing? *What if* you found restoration and redemption in Christ? *What if* your story was used to help another woman find salvation and an eternity in the realm of heaven? *What if* God created you with a plan? I'm writing this to tell you that He did. He has a purpose and a plan and He's giving you the courage to handle this. *What if you let Him?*

These are the seasons where growth happens. Where we grow closer to Christ. Firmer in our foundation and declaring with boldness our identity as daughters of the King. *This* is we where we fight the good fight and keep the faith (2 Timothy 4:7). But only if you *choose* to trust Him. Only if you *choose Him first.*

Coping mechanisms are vitally important to combat the lingering questions and confusing thoughts. Compartmentalizing is a tactic I have gained from therapy, and something, *years later,* I still work on almost daily. Compartmentalizing can be described therapeutically as placing your feelings or emotions in a box (metaphorically) in order to sort them out in a healthy transaction or work them out at a later date in time.

But when I find myself in conversation, I would describe it more like this: the process of being able to take my painful thoughts, memories, lingering questions, or concerns as they creep in, tell them, "Hey, I'll be back for you in a few hours," file them away for a while, and then allow myself the time to sit down later that evening, whether alone or with a trusted person, and sort out every last file.

I give myself an hour time frame. And when my hour is lapsed, I say, "I'm done for now." If I need to come back to those thoughts, I create the time and space for it. I have found it amazing how organizing our thought processes are imperative in healing both mentally and even physically. I can guarantee that it takes a little bit of leaning hard into. A little bit of struggle between doing it and meaning it and a lot of grace to sit down on a couch by yourself at night and talk it out (usually alone.) But hey, girl. *It. Works.*

Once I nailed my process down, I began sleeping better, focusing on my job and home life with more clarity, and even giving myself more opportunities to invest in extracurriculars because all of my time wasn't revolving around the constant negative emotions rattling around in my memories.

Before learning this treatment, I would wander around work or home aimlessly attempting to focus and control my brain. I even recall dropping my girls off with their father for a few hours and driving around aimlessly talking out my thoughts into thin air. Sometimes shouting it all out to God.

Getting the words out of your body is imperative to the healing process and mental health. It's especially healthy when you have a solid person speaking truth back at you in your rambling. Whether you find yourself within the beginning stages, the middle of the court process, or even after this nightmare has all ended, talk out loud. Seek out help and health in diverse forms. Don't hold it all inside. I cannot stress this enough, friend. Please find a safe and educated route to mental health.

We cannot allow a stigma of perfection to linger in our faith anymore. There is no shame in help.

If you want to succeed in despair, my friend, it will happen. Anger is often the road *well traveled*. Along the beaten path you will make many friends, some who will be named destruction and hate. Destruction takes over your home, maybe your finances. It seeps into your car and cell phone, into your conversations and routines until eventually it devours your thoughts and mental clarity. Destruction works best when instead of choosing forgiveness, we choose distance. Distance from healthy thoughts, healthy choices, healthy relationships with God and others. It will do exactly as it promises and continue to destroy what few pieces of your life are still intact.

Divorce is all too often the best friend to these diseases. If you wake up one day and realize that this is all happening, that you can't stop it or don't want to, that you're broken inside and considering letting the bitterness consume you, pause.

The book of Proverbs is full of paradigms on life lessons. Our pain isn't new to this world. People have been experiencing heartbreak and deceit and betrayal long before you and I were on this planet, girl. If you allow yourself to be overtaken by the destruction, you're giving into the devil's master plan to destroy your life. If only for a day, he will continue to give his all at chipping away your joy. Don't allow it. Instead, I would urge you to consider what 1 Peter promises all Christians will eventually endure. Verse 5:10 (NIV) states, *And the God of all grace, who called you to his eternal glory in Christ, after you have suffered a little while, will himself restore you and make you strong, firm and steadfast.*

"After you have suffered a little while" is probably not the phrase you wanted to read right now, but the beautiful part comes after: *"will himself restore you and make you strong, firm and steadfast."* I don't know how you've landed here in the bankruptcy sector of marriage like me. Wondering where it all went wrong and how to make it all right. But I do know that after the suffering and the confusion and the broken, there is most definitely strength and wholeness and restoration. And I'm here to tell you all about it.

Hate follows closely behind destruction. Like a bad taste in your mouth, it clears away the sweetness that once came from within. Hate sweeps up what destruction left behind. With foul language, no desire for hope, no love lost for the one destruction already destroyed, hate throws the final punch of the victims he chooses to deflate. Hate has been known to destroy families, friendships, marriages, work relations, finances, and often even divide countries against themselves.

Another dirty relative that tags along with doubt and destruction is the ugly trait known as depression. Ever heard of it? Felt it? Same, girl.

Without question, any level of anxiety you have experienced will reach a peak. Panic attacks, anxiety-riddled days. Mental health is necessary for every aspect of healing. And as someone who exhibited symptoms of post-traumatic stress within my divorce process, I can tell you firsthand that healthy is best. Let pride take a back seat here, friends.

Healthy minds beget healthy souls beget healthy bodies.

Sister, watch out for the side effects of divorce: doubt, depression, and anxiety. They seek us out just us a predator seeks their prey. They wait until you are most vulnerable, off your guard, unprepared. And then? They attack. Preparation is key. Watch for the warning signs. And in my honest opinion, get help even before they make their appearances. Trust me, you'll be so thankful that you did.

5

New Creation

How often do we as Christians really dwell on the death that Jesus bore on the cross? In my daily life (or unless it's Good Friday), I don't sit and dwell on the emotional and physical reality that was Christ's death. It's easy for us to go day-to-day not remembering His tortuous end, nor do I believe we ought to continually live in the sadness of that. After all, the Resurrection is the major plot point of the New Testament, further reminding us even more of why we ought to get out of the dwelling of sadness and into the fight for our lives for literal Christ's sake.

However, I do believe that we ought to, from time to time, recall that the pain Jesus experienced the day of His death was horrifying for a reason. We often forget that the burdens we carry in this life He also lived with and carried to His death—to ultimate death. I believe that in the anguish of the old rugged cross, my pain and your pain was etched in with His skin and blood and tears.

Growing up in a Baptist church and private school turned homeschooler, Bible lessons were my daily routine. I should've known better, but I'm ashamed to admit to you how many years I lived believing or thanking God that I wasn't present the day of Jesus's death. How could those horrible, terrible, no-good men do what they did to Him? Why would they spit on Him and mock Him? Why would they beat Him within an inch of His life and then make Him drag His cross to Calvary's hill with His skin hanging off of His bones?

They ripped His beard from His face. Didn't the people around Him want to help? Didn't they see they could protest? Why would they let this happen?

The subtlety of being naive. The truth though. Man does it hurt. The reality of it all is my failures, my broken marriage, the shame that I fight often of being a divorced woman and single mama, my heavy fear I carry of letting my family down, and the disappointment I was sure God had waiting for me—all of that was slashed into His skin with ropes woven with glass and nails. He wore a crown of dirty, splintered thorns that said *my* name (yours too.) Blunt-ended nails pierced through and shattered His bones with the same words of abuse that I will forever carry deep within my scars. His tears the night before as He prayed in the garden while His friends slept carelessly nearby spilled out for me and for you while He begged the Father to take the unfathomable legacy from Him, and all in the name of love. Because the truth is, I was there. I was the one shouting profanities at Him. I was the one spitting on Him and cursing Jesus's name. Mocking His title. "All Hail! King of the Jews!"

But even more than all of that, He wore the crown of thorns that would, thousands of years later, bear an uncanny resemblance to the shame that I could choose to carry even now for my failed marriage and brokenness. He did all of that for me, for you. He endured the abuse and the criticism and the anguish so that you and I would not have to live a life of defeat. But, and this is a superlative *but*, sister, when we choose to focus on our woes, on our own failures, and our own setbacks in this life, when we allow the voice of defeat and shame to whisper the lies that we are a slave to our failures, we are taking our eyes off of the cross that already bore it all. Furthermore, when we as believers take our pain into our own hands, when we attempt to medicate our wounds first and alone with anything other than truths and God's healing words, we are attempting surgery that only the Master Surgeon can perform. But *most* importantly, we're taking our eyes off of the empty tomb.

You see, the tomb was the dwelling place of Jesus for a short three days. What should've been an eternal resting place for a physical being was instead used as a transformative juncture for a spiritual awakening. Within its walls it held all of the darkness the world could ever imagine. And yet still, the light could not be contained.

History scarcely tells us of the loss that His family and friends felt. But can you just imagine being there as they laid Him alone in that dark room? Put yourself in the shoes of the disciples as they watched their innocent friend being gruesomely murdered. Ask anyone who has lost someone dear to them. When it's all over, when the crowd is gone, when the room is quiet, the pain of the physical loss is nearly unbearable. Can you imagine having watched those three days unfold? Watching Him suffer betrayal at the hands and kiss of His best friend, watching them wrongfully accuse Him and sentence him to a public and humiliating death of the worst kind. I can assure you, that three days didn't feel short to Jesus's friends. It didn't feel like a quick weekend. No.

For the disciples, the tomb was dark and cold. It was lonely and forsaken. It was a place where they laid their friend. Unsure of what was next and why it was all happening. Isn't that so like pain? Isn't that the description of shame, of guilt, of disappointment? Those things are hidden deep in dark places that no one else can see into. They whisper secrets to us that we dare not speak out loud for fear of their truths.

"I'm not good enough. I'm a fraud. Is this all my fault? I will never find another man who loves me. There is no Christian guy who wants to go out with a divorced woman or single mom. Why would anyone listen to me? I can't be a leader. I'm a failure, I'm a sinner. My family, my church, my friends will be so disappointed in me. I cannot control my anxiety. I need to be a better Christian."

The lies, friends! The lies! They are the tombs of death that take us away from the eternal light and mercies of Jesus. They are the thieves of our healthy mentalities and peaceful souls and able bodies, and they seek to steal the joy that only our heavenly Father can ever truly provide. I know it hurts so much in the darkness. I know the pit of failure is so low sometimes that it would just be easier to stay in depression and not even want to crawl out of it. Confusion settles in and makes that same web of deceit that we know brings more questions than answers. But wait.

Be still.

What if we took those same previous questions and thoughts, the ones that keep us awake at night and seek to steal our peace, and we flipped them on their side? Let's turn them around. Do a 180.

What if instead of crying yourself to sleep at night, you whispered your heart to the Father as you fall into slumber? *What if* instead of being codependent on the memories that both make you and break you, you sit with a friend or therapist and find healing and restoration and new adventures? Journal your memories. But place them on a shelf. And move on.

What if instead of depriving yourself or disciplining yourself for a bad choice, you opened the Word and read a psalm of praise? *What if* your heart's countenance changed dramatically within minutes of lifting your hands to worship music? *What if* it's all possible? It's all probable. It's all profound.

The pain doesn't have to own you anymore. The brokenness is not how Christ wants you to live this life. How can we live in shame or regret and pain but teach the gospel message? The fact is, it's not possible to do both.

"No man can serve two masters" (Matthew 6:24).

Remember, *"Many are the plans in a man's heart, but the Lord directs his steps"* (Proverbs 19:21).

If you had told me this would be my story, I would've called you crazy. I would shake my head, giggle a little, and say, "Who, me? You've got the wrong girl." This was *never* going to be my story. *It was never going to be me.*

I'm just a small-town girl. My grandpa was my pastor, and my family is a staple in our community. I grew up behind the scenes in church. I've made pretty good life choices (spoiler: comparing myself unattractively to others here). I go to church every Sunday, I serve in several facets, I tithe regularly, I got good grades in school, I was the first in my family to go to college, I got my degree with honors, I made my family proud, I married a great guy... Not me, nope, you've got the wrong girl. (Jokes on me!)

But seriously, sister, can you relate?

Well, here I am. And here you are. Strangers on two sides of a book page, trying to understand the unraveling of our lives. We may never understand the demise of our marriage. That is a struggle that dwelled within me for far longer than I care to admit, but there's also a sense of relief and calming that comes to your soul when you stop fighting the control to understand. Faith deepens when you lay down your inability to make sense of it all and trust that Christ still has plans to prosper you. He doesn't say He has plans sometimes or maybe or *only if* conditionally or legalistically. He says He has plans to prosper us. That's it. And I choose to believe that when we willingly lay down our crosses, surrender to Him in the attempt to align our will with His, He makes good on this promise to us. And the freedom that breaks the chains of defeat when we accept the truth over the lies? Free. Oh, how *free* indeed.

Recall that last part of the story, that part where the miracle happened, and the world would never again be the same? That is imperative to our story too.

Not only because, of course, death is defeated, heaven is open, the veil is torn. But what that means for us on this side of eternity. The *overlap*: where we still live in the anguish and sin. Where salvation is promised yet sin is too. Let's revisit that empty tomb together. Let's go there. Let's bring our faults and our fears into the grave and then release them to the Father, turn around, and clinging to the robe of the Perfect One, walk out of that tomb of darkness into the world declaring that we are a new creation.

"Therefore if anyone is in Christ, the new creation has come: The old has gone, the new is here!" (2 Corinthians 5:17).

Divorce often feels just like death. Don't expect to just hand your pain over to God and wake up the next morning completely healed. Much like the aching of a phantom pain, the severing ties left from divorce take time to heal. It's a process. I'm not saying that daily progress isn't felt or isn't a step in the right direction here. But what you will experience or already have is that this is a process of grief. Allow it. Allow every difficult stage and hour to come and then experience it with as much clarity as you can possibly give it.

I recall my therapist describing grief as a mountain, often drawing a little sketch to show me where she thought I was in the process. (Remember here how impatience is my strong suit?) I wanted to barrel through the stages, conquer them with ease, and prove to everyone (mostly myself) that I was capable. Capable to overcome the abuse, the lies, and the internal pain in order to be stronger and better. I-am-woman-hear-me-roar-kind of mentality. Stupid, I know. That's not to say I'm now not stronger and wiser and more empathetic.

But God had different plans. Instead, He had plans to take His time with me. To teach me true, unconditional, unadulterated, and pure love within the healing process. And binding up wounds? Well, that takes more time than I wanted to admit to myself.

My counselor always knocked me back down a few cliffs when she would say I needed to work on this or that issue weighing heavily on me. The thing that took me hardest to comprehend was accepting the length of time the process of grief and healing can actually take. Everyone will experience each stage differently and in different time frames. Sister, do not rush this. You are in each stage of grief for a reason. Each season has a diverse opportunity for growth that the previous did not and the future will not. Live in the stage you are in right now as mundane, painful, aching as it might be. Tell God exactly how you feel right there in your lowest valley and lay it down for Him to carry. Before you know it, you'll be scaling the mountain and looking back down at the growth you've achieved, all the while feeling closer to Christ if you continually rely on Him as your harness.

Here's where the really good news happens. Are you ready? Are you excited? I am!

"Rejoice in hope."

Ever heard of that? Romans 12:12 is a verse that is engraved in my heart.

Without hope for the future, without laughing in the face of it like that Proverbs woman, what is the point of all this? I think that's exactly why God gave us that description of the Proverbs 31 woman. She laughs without fear of the future. Then Romans: she rejoices in hope. Do you have hope for your future? What does that look like to you? Go ahead, write it down. All of it. Tell a friend, a mentor, your therapist. Tell God all about it. Guess what, girl? He already knows. He already sees into those deep desires of what you're afraid to say out loud. Would you believe it if I said He actually wrote that in your heart? I think He smiles when we bring those secrets back to Him. Like a father delighting in his children's brutal honesty, knowing they have no idea what lies ahead. Prosperity, sister. That's what lies ahead. Believe it.

The tomb was such a dark place until it wasn't anymore. Until one day, the waiting was over.

Grief was defeated. The rock rolled away and the angels appeared and Jesus asked all nonchalantly like He didn't already know, "Why are you crying?"

That's it. Right there. One day, friend, you will wake up and this nightmare will have just been a terrible chapter in your story, a part of your life. But don't you believe for one second that this is it. That it's all over. *No.* This is just your three days. Your lonely, dark hours where you have to choose to keep the faith and remember in all of it that He promised us this is not the end. Pain, humiliation, and brokenness, don't to be the final words here. No matter the weight you carry for being divorced in the culture of Christianity, God simply does not want you to carry that cross anymore. Leave that fear and abuse, the shame and betrayal behind you. Whatever measures of defeat are interwoven into the fibers of your story, lay them down in the tomb and wait for the rock to roll away. Because it will.

Your day is coming. Your resurrection from this purgatory has already been ordained and fought for. Friend, pain is a dwelling place that Jesus doesn't want you to be in. A tomb. And just like Jesus, we can rise from it. Your story, much like mine, doesn't end in the tomb, my friend. The story of new life is only beginning.

I can tell you all of this is true. In my deepest hours of brokenness, I had to choose, repeatedly, to believe with faith that there is indeed more. That God remains in control of this. That He will show up. And guess what? He did. And know what else? He still does. Even when I forget that He's there weaving an intricate web of details for my life, plans, and a future for me and my daughters, He's right there showing Himself to me in sovereignty and reminding me that all along, He never forgot what I asked of Him.

It's not easy to wait. It's stinking hard to continually lay it down when we want to do it our way, fulfill our own desires and our own happiness. "I got this, God." Trust me, I've swung and missed more than once. But grace is always there showing up to remind me that what He has is always better. My pastor reminded our congregation recently of God's continual workings in our lives. How often it feels like much difference isn't being made for the kingdom when we are at our lowest points or even in the basic structure of normal life. But in fact, God is continually working in our lives in order to fulfill His kingdom.

"Don't miss that Jesus' work in the Present points to a greater work in the future" (Pastor N. Gatzke 2018).

Even in the darkness, sister, when you can barely breathe let alone pray, simply go to Him. Ask for His will. And then ask Him for your desires. Abide in His words, and when your heart aligns with God's will, you can be sure He will be there for it. And so will I. Cheering you on. Expecting your story to turn into your testimony. Furthering the kingdom together because you chose to believe that God is good. All the time. Even in the valleys.

6

Reality

Reliving the demise of my marriage and the elements leading up to my divorce is trying for me. It's not something I ever desire to remember. The memories inside me often fight over themselves from good to bad, bantering like a ping-pong war for the sole purpose of confusion. Honestly, I'm also never quite sure how much I should offer up when speaking about it. Some tell me this dissipates as the years progress; others tell me it's a lifelong battle even after moving on.

It might best be described as asking me to rip open one of those wounds that's been stitched shut, healed now, but still tender to the touch. From being served papers not just once but twice thanks to a postal error, from a failed dissolution to a cold courtroom sitting across the table from the man I vowed to love and cherish above myself, the memories are tragic. Often the only way I describe divorce to those near to me is that of a death. The truth is that I actually believe it's probably meant to be that way. Part of you dies. A piece of you that you will never again live in the same form. Innocence has been shed. Which brings me to some cold, hard truths.

God hates divorce. It's true. I cringe writing this for several reasons. I know critics will tear it apart. (And between you and me, I do *not* handle criticism too well. It's a growth point, am I right?) I know the legalists will shout "Amen!" from the rooftops. But the fact is, two opposing sides of the fence with their opinions won't stop me from saying this to you. Don't get me wrong; opinions often matter. Often they don't. But those shouts from the sidelines aren't my biggest fears. They won't stop me from speaking the truth that your wounded heart needs to hear the most.

My biggest fear is that you, my dear friend, will read those words from the book of Malachi or hear them in a study or be on the receiving end of harsh, opinionated legalists and believe that because of them, God doesn't accept you or even want you anymore for the scars that you carry or for the *scarlet D* you wear stitched on your shoulder. And, dear girl, there is absolutely nothing further from grace and the truth. I believe that. And yes, that verse is in His Word, black and white. God hates divorce. I'm not arguing with the Word of God and challenging Christian culture to tear this apart. But I do believe that we ought to look at it God's way—the grace way—instead of with blatant condemnation.

Divorce was never supposed to be part of the master plan for our lives. Nowhere does God verbalize that He hates the divorcee. But rather, He hates the *act of* divorce. He hates what that destruction means for His children. He hates that a good and perfect union can be broken, that man is tearing apart what He has joined together. Marriage can be and ought to be beautiful. Marriage was created to be a partnership. A union between man and woman who both bring traits and strengths into a commitment to lean onto each other. Two people who might also bring their pain and sinful nature in the attempt to better one another, to build each other up with encouragement, to walk closer to God and each other in the journey of marriage.

But then something happened. Something called Eden. Where we took what *should have been* and ruined it for all of humanity. And that's where we are right now.

What *should have been* is often where we find ourselves stuck, isn't it? My marriage *should have* made it. My kids *should have* gotten the chance to grow up in a healthy home, where mom and dad work their problems out peacefully, not where one parent attacks and assaults the other. My heart *should have* been safe. But it wasn't. We live in a broken world where broken hearts exist. Broken vows exist. Broken people exist.

Let's take the Scriptures where God reminds us that He hates divorce and instead of feeling only shame in those words, look in the mirror and say, "Yes, me too.

"I hate divorce. I hate that it exists. I hate that my heart is shattered. I hate that my family is no longer whole. I hate that my children carry this legacy. I hate the brutality and the suffering that we must endure through the trials within.

"But God doesn't hate me. He didn't want this for me simply because He desires to see me whole. He wants to see me joyful and at peace. He wants my meditation to be on His kingdom and His promises."

We're supposed to be becoming more like Him on this adventure called life, right? So let's do that. The next time we hear the words "*God hates divorce,*" we can simply reply with, "*Yes. He hates divorce. And that's okay because so do I.*"

Once you've experienced the sharing of your entire being with another person, that separation doesn't dissipate overnight. The truth of the matter is that just because the papers are signed and the gavel is slammed, the reality of divorce, all of its repercussions, takes ample time to cope with. You will never again be the same woman. Your life will never be what it once was. You will be a new woman and that takes time and faith and tears.

But God still wants you. Even if you're wondering why your marriage is shattered or your spouse decides you aren't enough for him anymore, the greatest example of true love is Christ walking alongside us, seeing us in the pain of divorce, and still saying, "Here I Am, daughter. I want to love you. I want to heal you. I'm the greatest love you'll ever truly know. Here I Am. Choose me."

It's time to fall in love again. Time to experience the fulfillment that comes from love Himself. That there is no love greater, no love fuller, no love more accepting than Jesus seeing us in our most battered, ugly, painful moments that no one else can even witness and still He's choosing to love. It's time.

Vulnerability 101: If I had a dollar for every time I have cried out to God, "But I don't want to be alone!" well, I would be sitting on a warm beach somewhere writing this book to you instead of a cold house in gray-skies Ohio. I often remind myself that the deepest desires of our hearts are the ones God has given us. So how can my life's greatest desire to be a wife, to be a blessing and encourager and promoter and lover and best friend to a good man, and yet here I am. Single. Alone. No prospects in sight. Christian Mingle's looking better by the day!

Okay, seriously though, sweet sister, remember those baby steps? And I'm preaching to myself here too. Remember God's timing? Part of saying we believe in God's divine timing is relinquishing control over our desires. So take a big breath. You didn't fall in love in one day. And your marriage won't feel over just because the papers are signed.

Many women rush into new relationships because it's just so hard to be alone. I get it. I totally get it. But something God had placed in my heart within my journey as a single woman, something I'm still learning daily, is that I don't need a man to complete me, but of course I desire a man to complement me. God knows this. I feel the longing for companionship—to meet someone and spoil them. Someone to call and talk about our days. Someone who I can encourage and can encourage me. Someone who won't mind the scars I carry and will dress my wounds with caution and gentleness. Maybe someone with fears of his own or deep wounds that I can hold and remind him of God's plan for him too. Someone to hold up when they're down, to pray with in the day-to-day, someone to (try) golf with, someone to laugh until I snort with, someone to cry with in the pangs of life…

I could go on for days, but the truth is, I don't know what lies ahead for me and you. But I do know that God does not forsake us. If he has a future, healthy, God-ordained relationship for me, then that's amazing! And if not, well, I'll still have to choose to trust that He knows exactly what He's doing in the (what feels like) mundane realities of this life. And no matter which road He has for us in the future, *He is still so good.*

The desire to fulfill our own futures and say, "Okay, God, I can take it from here," is always possible, right? But what if (just for a second) I tell God what I want and then I get it? What if this crazy, out-of-this-world desire that I have is fulfilled by a great Christian man? Then what? Will I choose to be content then? Will I ever really be happy with having what I've wanted and begged and waited for? Will I wake up and say, "Okay, God, I'm never asking you for anything ever again because I have exactly what I want now?"

No. I won't. To be content in all circumstances as Paul charges us with (Philippians 4:11) is in all possibilities the hardest of realities for us as mere humanity to ever cope with. The fact of the matter is, it doesn't matter what it is or how badly I want it. But it does matter what I do with what *God has already* entrusted to me. In our sorrow and loneliness, there is contentment that can only be wholly fulfilled by Jesus. That's what we ought to be striving toward. To have faith so rooted in the understanding of eternity and the implications of what that means for our lives here that we ought to shift focus instead of using our current realities to further build His kingdom.

In brutal honesty, I have suffered terrible seasons of ungratefulness, always wanting more, to move from this moment or season, to be done with brokenness, to be completely restored, and to be painstakingly honest. Often, I have longed to catch a glimpse of my life ten years from now. As if to say my life could be better, happier, healthier, or that I'll even be here on this side of glory. There are zero promises for this thinking. Contentment is something to strive for, yes, and in the hardest moments realize that we as mortals won't always reach it. Pick ourselves back up from our angst. Give ourselves the grace God has preordained, and seek out contentment in Christ even more.

No amount of earthly possessions (i.e., homes, cars, jewels, social media followers, career changes, shoes, makeup, technology, or relationships) will satisfy our longing that we have deep inside for innate peace. Jesus is the only way, the only truth, and the only life that will well up our souls and hearts with His ultimate peace and keep us on the path of righteousness.

But how? How are we supposed to practice contentment in the longing? In the midst of singleness when we desire for a spouse? How do we practice contentment when the bills are piling up, and we feel overwhelmed by the demands of financial responsibility? How do we practice contentment when we're the only parent discipling and shepherding and waking to fevered children and still have all the tasks of life waiting eagerly on our doorsteps?

The answer is still, and always will be, Jesus. We come to Him. We talk to Him in our lonely hours. When we look for more? Look to the heavens. When we don't want to feel alone? Tell him of our desire for connection. Find healthy friends, women who know how you feel; seek their friendship. Allow God to form you in other ways right now. I believe there is a season for everything. Just as Ecclesiastes says, *"For everything there is a season…a time to break down, and a time to build up. A time to weep, and a time to laugh, a time to mourn and a time to dance…"*

And that is just so like this life that you and I are living. A season for pain, of heartbreak, of tragedy… But that same season will inevitably shift to a season for joy, because remember in Psalm 30:5, *"Weeping endures for a night, but joy comes in the morning."*

I am but a weak and frail human. The flesh will want what it wants, but the soul? Only the deepest of desires can ever be fully satisfied with the union of Christ. I will always ask for more. I will always need, want, desire for something out of this life. Because that's my heart's nature. God knows this. But you and I have to seek Christ with our entire being. Saturate ourselves first with the never-ending unconditional love of the heavenly Father and only then, if He sees fit, can we ever even consider the possibility of moving on with any other man postdivorce. There is no one who will ever love you, understand you, or complete you more wholly than Jesus Christ himself.

One more thought on this topic, though, that I need to share with you in this moment for sake of self-preservation. Whatever lonely season haunts you, whatever sadness sneaks into your soul begging for validation, just don't rush out and date to hush the screaming that is reminding you of being single. All too often, I see

Christian women lost within the throngs of divorce already out and about dating new men before healing has even had a chance to take root. Often before the paperwork is anywhere near final.

Now, my opinions don't much matter, but if you've read this far, I have to believe you find solidarity in some of what I've entrusted you with. So please, if you choose, take it or leave it from me here, but I do not believe God would condone this. The struggle for God-given companionship is authentic. We were created for each other. But wise choices were never made on an emotional whim. And seeking out men to fulfill our human desires—especially when we are deep in the midst of vulnerability, aching to our cores—will never end in a healthy relationship or greener pastures on the other side of this.

Instead, let me encourage you that when the nights are far too long, choose to pick up your cross and your Bible. Sit down in the quietness (and the loneliness) and read Scripture. Find a trustworthy woman or friend to study the same chapters as you and find accountability in a weekly plan to discuss it. From experience, I can share with you that these are the very moments that Christ uses to mend our hearts. He uses His words to show us the path. He lights the way and carries us through the darkness, but He won't do it if you don't choose to follow Him. Often, we get mad when we don't *hear* God or see His hand present. But are we actively looking and listening? Sister, don't forget that we are called to follow Him. Even when things are good, even when things are bad, pick up that Bible. Read. Pray. Talk out loud to God.

Call me crazy, but I started talking out loud to God throughout my day—in my car, in the shower, folding laundry. And you know what? He listens! He soaks up every conversation I have with Him because He wants to hear from me. He wants to hear from you too! He wants this time with us to develop our relationship with Him. How do you cultivate relationships with the people around you? Conversation! Why would it be any different with Jesus?

When you take your time and thoughts captive, you will notice a change in your demeanor, actions, and thoughts. God wants to replace that void in your life. Let Him.

This is why it's so important for us to practice for the sake of contentment. This season of struggle is for spiritual exercise. Exercising our faith in ways that we might never get to walk out again. Take this tough time frame, catch your breath, and walk through the drought declaring to learn something—anything—beneficial from it so that someday, way ahead in our future, you and I might look back at this *night of weeping* and say, *"Wow, I really hated that season. But will you look and see what God did there? Right there in that moment?"*

He is constantly and continually fashioning a way to complete a good work within us. That work will never be final until the day we reach His throne, but for now, let's give Him the keys to our satisfaction and allow Him to enter our gates that have been hardened with cynicism and resentment. Only He can teach us forgiveness through His unfailing grace and turn it into something profound for His glory. Remember, for every season, there is a reason.

Contentment is by far the hardest struggle of my virtues. It's much less work to be unhappy in the day-to-day. But in the end? It's me and Christ. *"For me to live is Christ, to die is gain."*

Let's lay down the burden of our struggle at the cross, a thousand times over if we must, and believe in hope. Just as the *"grass withers and the flowers fall, the Word of God endures forever."* Our seasons will never stay the same for long. But Jesus. He is constant. And unwavering. And never changing.

I hope for so much more. Do you? But my ultimate hope, oh all of that is in God.

"Amazing Grace...how [truly] sweet the sound."

7

Counsel

A wise man listens to advice.

—Proverbs: 12:15

Sister, the input I'm going to share with you now is some of the most important part of this story. Don't skip over it. Don't over analyze it. Do take it with importance and follow through. I can promise you this—your future much healthier and stronger self will thank you for doing it.

Before my separation ever began and I knew I was floundering in my marriage, I reached out to some safe women in my community. (They happened to be friends from church in my case, but I recognize that isn't always the same possibility for everyone.) Whatever you do, please, don't reach out to friends that aren't healthy in their faith walk. If you want one hundred friends to back you and give you gusto, they're easy to find. They're also the same ones who will send you into a spiral of chaos and drop off soon after the high of the drama dissipates, leaving you more wrecked than you already are.

But one good friend, oh one solid girl who will stand with you in the fire and speak affirmation and hard truths is much harder to find, but she is worth her weight in gold. You might not find her right away, you might find her on this road well traveled, or you might meet her in a mom group or through a counselor. Whatever you do, do not let her go. Friendships are forged in the fire. In my case, I knew some trusted women from my small groups that I could confide in. I didn't need to speak details to these friends; I simply had to ask and say that I needed the name of a trusted counselor who could help me in my marital troubles. They didn't ask questions. Instead, they led me to water.

It wasn't long after I sought counsel that I found myself directly within separation. Perhaps you can check off this same list of personality traits? I was so shocked I didn't tell people around me other than immediate family for weeks. I was ashamed. Scared. Emotionally beaten. Anxiety riddled, unhealthy physically, suffering PTSD, barely sleeping, and poorly performing at my job. Keeping my eyes open to deal with reality was excruciating yet sleeping only brought on more tears and loneliness. Thinking back to those months, I'm amazed that my own self made it out mentally alive, but more importantly, my soul found a peace greater than any relationship can ever give me.

I'm not tooting my own horn when I say replaying the past is parallel to watching a friend of mine fight for her life and being so proud of her for her walk and the woman she is now. (I pray this for you, too, sister.) How did that happen? Who is this person in the mirror now? Me. But a stronger, mentally healthy, wiser woman who is much more aware of her self-worth.

A woman who is chosen, redeemed, loved. Who is worth more than rubies. A daughter of the risen King who binds up my wounds and refines me like gold. A mother who will fight for her children and refuse for her daughters to watch how a woman ought not to be treated. Sister. So are you. You are chosen. You are redeemed. And most importantly, because I KNOW your heart does not believe this truth enough…YOU ARE LOVED.

Soak in the goodness of love. Pure and true. Never ceasing. Never betraying. Never forsaking. Sometimes, I wonder what that looks like here on earth. We hear it all the time at weddings, but I don't think we can fully understand the depth of those words in the Father's grand scheme for us. Unconditional in all His promises. Forsaking his throne in the heavenly realm to show us how much He actually loves us. God calls you, friend.

He doesn't need you. But I can assure you, He does want you.

Counsel always seemed like such a dirty word to me. As I said before, I grew up in a small Baptist church. My grandfather was my pastor and my parents did pretty much everything in the church. That was just my norm. But counsel was that word that was only used for people in really dark places. Secrets and pain. Things twenty years ago we dared not even discuss.

Today they're almost trends in the current church age. We've shifted a lot from that place in the church's progression. For the good, mostly. And I am so very thankful for this. My opinion of counsel is that it could easily be abused. It's not a place for us to sit and share our life stories and walk out a few pounds mentally lighter. It could certainly help in that area, but I believe true counseling is to be used for sound biblical advice. For reprimand. For the purpose of reforming us into new creatures so that we may continue pursuing God's purpose for us in a healthier state.

Okay, here's that really great wisdom I'm trying to get to you. Find. A. Christian counselor. Not just a faith-based counselor working outside of the realm of a church, but a counselor working within the structure of accountability who will guide you according to the Scriptures. Please, don't run away screaming because I'm using the terms some might read as *organized religion*. I'm only acknowledging and claiming the fact here that as Christians who undoubtedly come from many diverse backgrounds, I believe that a therapist practicing within the boundaries of a safe and reliable foundation will be able help you along your way.

Sometimes this is not the case. And unfortunately, in a world where churches are often no longer a safe haven from abuse but often housing the abusers (my heart is broken over the reality that some churches negate this privilege and hurt their patrons even more unintentionally), we can't afford to live in a world where the one safe haven we should have is the same place the devil will use to divide us. Honestly, don't give up heart finding a woman who can guide you, pray with you, and love you through this. I'm talking Bible out, prayer happening, ain't no shame in loving Jesus out loud, girls.

I know a trustworthy counsel is hard to find. Sometimes you need to visit a few before you commit. But listen, Do. Not. Follow.

Your. Heart. As trivial as this might sound, following your head and instincts and hopefully reviews of other people before you delve deep into counsel will remind you that you are there for growth, answers, and clarity. Once you find your person, do it. Don't quit going. And *don't just talk. Listen.*

When I walked into my first session, awkward would be the right term to describe the atmosphere. "How does this work? What do I say?" come to mind. It feels sort of like a doctor's appointment mixed with a principal's visit (only at first though, don't lose me). And then…the goodness. She listened with earnest ears. She guided my thoughts with ease. She reminded me of God's joy waiting for me. The trying times were those that I asked the hard questions. "Is this normal? Do I go back? What changes am I looking for? Did I do the right thing? Is this grief? Why am I calm? Why am I mad? How long will I be sad? How do you know this isn't different? What if you're wrong? When will I feel better / sleep more / enjoy life again?"

With grace and tenderness, she answered every single thought. And then she lifted me up in all my messy glory in prayer and for sanctification. The thing with counseling, dear girl, is this. Don't you even step foot in that room if you don't plan to heed advice from those wiser than you. There will come a point where you think you know everything better than those around you. You think you'll have it mapped out, how the cookie is gonna crumble. You might even tell yourself things like "They're going to be wrong. He was different. This time was different. Our story will change. He's not really this person? I have to act how? Wait, I need to do what? How did this happen to me? I was never going to be this person."

All before the final conclusion: "*My story wasn't supposed to end this way.*"

It won't go as you planned, I promise. Your spouse won't agree like he said, and your original plans to keep it all going smoothly without any more turmoil will—without a doubt—falter. Ask me how I know.

Right in the smack-dab middle of my divorce, as my heart was crumbled, the relationships around me were aching with me; and for me, my feelings, I had no feelings left to hurt. My brother encouraged me with some of the most simplistic yet profound advice I've never been able to shake. Allow me to share it with you too. He said, "Sissy (because the best brothers still call their little sisters *sissy*; it's endearing), *you are in the middle of a war. A bad one. But you? You will find the will to be strong if you lean on God, and God? He's got this thing already beat. Remember something. You can't have a victory without a war.*"

Oh, the goodness. Say it with me. *"You can't have a victory without first having the war."*

Remember a while back when I told you to brace yourself for this? Put on your armor? This is where it all starts weaving into intricate place. Counsel is a highly important aspect in putting on your armor. Wise individuals around you can help gird you with truth, righteousness, prepare you to share the gospel of peace, grow your faith, solidify the foundation of your salvation, and speak God's word over you and with you. Every aspect of Ephesians 6:14–16 speaks to preparing for battle. Christ only wants one outcome for you, warrior woman. And that is victory. *Declare it. Do it. Own it.*

Believing that God honors His children's requests is something that I struggle with. Personally, and from my experiences, I believe the difficulty of this concept has more to do with the reality that God can in fact do whatever it is that we ask of Him. Faith is after all the substance of things we hope for. Believing that God is omnipotent and able. The harsher reality is recognizing that we do not always get what we want simply because we ask, beg, and plead for it. Faith though, it's not true faith if it's only good enough for us when things are going our way. Faith is what happens when we realize sometimes He says yes, but if not, He really is still good.

Several years before my divorce, when my daughters were only infants, the Lord directed my steps into a local group of young mothers who meet several times a month known as MOPS (Mothers of Preschoolers). Without hesitation and to this very day, I tell every new young mom I cross paths with to find a moms group in a local church and join it. Little did I know that my joining this group was God directing my steps into a safety net of women who would not so far down the road harbor me, lay hands and pray over me, encourage me, and go to battle in prayer for me even within their own homes. These women loved on me in ways I never knew friends could. They became the women I would cry with, belly laugh with, vent to, rejoice with, and sometimes just be still with.

Equally as astounding to me was the group of older women known to me as *mentor moms* who would play a role in my future, several of whom were divorced and remarried. I never knew their stories until my own became my reality. They were the women who made sure I was surviving, made sure I was eating and sleeping, made sure we were sitting in church every Sunday, and reminded me that even when you hit rock bottom, Christ is in fact the rock at the bottom.

And one step further? When it felt like I was at the end, when I couldn't even imagine that there was more for my life, they were there to remind me that God wasn't done with me just yet. When I felt a huge scarlet *D* embellished on my shoulder, they were the women reminding me that shame is not a cross for me to carry. When I felt betrayed and broken, hoping for more, the words, "No, not yet, I have something better" were given as advice to wait upon the Lord and His providential timing.

I cry as I write from my heart the encouragement that each and every one of these women has been to my life. Many of them wouldn't even know the regard I hold for them. They hold a special corner inside of me that will never be erased. Often, I consider where I might be if I had tried to survive the brutality of divorce without this family by my side, and the sheer thought of waging that war without them can send me in to depression. My prayer warriors. My huntresses. My sisters.

They are necessary to lift you to the Father's throne when you are too weak to stand there yourself.

Do not be afraid to ask for help. Ask for friends to pray for you. And whatever you do, no matter how hard it is, be honest, find a good friend, and tell her the truth of what's happening in your life. You cannot walk this path alone. Find your tribe. They will be the ones walking into that fiery furnace with you and coming out untouched on the other side.

8

Recollections

Sister, if you and I were best friends sitting over some coffee and pie (because all good conversations happen over coffee where I come from), I might share all the gory and gruesome details of my divorce with you. But those details are not what this book is about. This is not a therapy session where I tell you all the bad things about my life and you agree over and over about how awful this world is and we laugh together and cry together and then probably go get a pedicure together. Instead, God has given me the words to write this story in the attempt to reach one weary woman's soul. A plea for you to come running to Him, whether you have been near to the cross and surrendering your heart or as far as the prodigal, lost and alone wandering back home. He desires you. He chooses you. He sees your pain and is asking you to bring it to Him so that He can carry this detestable, debilitating load for you.

My journal is filled with amazing stories about how God showed up for me in the divorce process. Hours over coffee would be filled with tears of both joy and pain as I recall them. But for now, just a portion of my story will suffice.

...and because of His faithfulness to me, I owe Him the glory of a life that will sing praises to His name.

As we were heading into one of many mediations, my soul was weary. Allow me to preface this as I feel pretty naive in my simplistic knowledge and under-standing of the court system. Lawyers operate under the guise that we know what family counseling, mediation, guardians, and legal jargon actually are. If you are entering the court process, might I rec-ommend you take a few hours and research what every process actu-ally means before you enter into them. Often, I left feeling defeated simply because I was wrong about what I thought was going to hap-pen in those rooms. You are already hurting and confused; don't add more stress to yourself than necessary. My personal counselor was well versed in proceedings and prepped me emotionally for what I now recognize as the damage that can be done right within the very walls of a courthouse.

Things happen there that ought never exist. Lies are told. Manipulations had. Unions both bound and broken, all under one roof. Courthouses will forever be a place of dread for me. A place where my anxiety will undoubtedly be triggered without repentance. I walked in there as two people, but I left as one. My body tired, my heart hurting as I sat across the hallway (from my soon-to-be ex-husband). The third floor of the courthouse was loud as people scurried up and down marble staircases. Entering and exiting ele-vators. Briefcases opened and shut. Papers shuffled. Plaintiffs and defendants hushing discussions back and forth in secrecy. What a morbid scene this was. Tragic.

To the right corridor there was a menial, one-stall bathroom. No updates in the thirty years I had been alive. They're made that way on purpose I suppose. After all, the people whose next stop might be jail don't have an easy out through a window or vent. Or worse. Even the stalls had no locks. Hard chairs and wooden benches resembling old-style church pews were the only seating choices, as if to punish every parishioner of the courthouse.

"Don't get comfortable here," they whisper.

"Don't worry I won't," I whisper to myself.

I pull my Bible app out on my phone. As I look around, I see most people drowning in a sea of addictive technology. Social media. An easy escape from reality when turmoil is heavy in the air. You could cut the tension in this hallway with a dull knife. Probably even plastic. I watch the people coming up and down the corridors. I wonder what their stories are. Are they similar to me? Have they been here before? Did they do something wrong to land them here? Or are they possibly just fighting for freedom from pain like myself? I watch their attorneys greet them as advocates one by one. Numbers, barely names. Making eye contact is awkward. "Don't judge me, and I won't judge you." We seem to agree without ever saying a word. I glance up at the man I'm legally bound to still—even—yet. It's a strange feeling.

I want to be with him. No, I want to be with the one who promised to honor and cherish me. Not attack and verbally assault me. I have to remind myself to keep my heart under wraps. It's what got me here in the first place. I feel the pang of unromantic love as I catch him look up at me. This isn't the same man. I wonder whether he is the same person I once would've given my life for.

But here he is. The one who screamed profanities in my face. Calling me words that I dare not utter because although they are long behind me, they still find a way into my blood as they bite like venom. Vulgarities that ache deep in the quiet corners of my heart. Words that singe the chords of my innermost being. That's the thing with love. You never really know if it's real until it's too late to give it and until it's too late to take it back.

The funny thing is, I wouldn't take it back. None of it. I chose to love him. I haven't figured it out. If maybe he's just changed or if maybe he was always this way. Was I (and everyone else) manipulated? I digress. After all, I don't need to have it all figured out. Some things just aren't my job. I bow my head as if to avoid his contact.

"What do you want me to read, Lord?"

Philippians.

I open my app and find the faithful chapter 4. Something stopped me though. I never made it to the popular verse 13. Instead, 6 and 7 beckoned me. The words jumbled under my breath as the Lord recited them back to me, *"Let your reasonableness be made known to all men. Do not be anxious about anything. But in everything by prayer and supplication with thanksgiving let your requests be made known to God.*

"And the peace of God which surpasses all understanding will guard your hearts and minds in Christ Jesus."

The Holy Spirit stopped me right there. I couldn't read more. I couldn't read less. Just the same two verses playing over in my mind as I sat in that stifling hallway aching to run away. Like a broken record, again, *"Let your reasonableness be made known to all men. The Lord is at hand."* This verse will be burned into my being for the rest of my days. Because what happened in the next three hours in a little square room in the middle of a disgusting divorce shook me to my core.

The secretary opened the room; we follow. The man who once opened every door for me, who waited until I went first, jumped ahead of me every time. Again. Manipulation. I scurry in behind and approach the mediator with a respectable demeanor. Half choking back tears, shaking like a frail leaf clinging to every last thread of a limb in late October. I sit alone. No attorneys present at this meeting. Only my estranged husband across from me with a smirk that says everything I need to know.

Here we are. You did this. Congratulations. You should've toughed this out. (I know these are his thoughts because he said these things to me on many occasions.) *I want to scream out loud. I couldn't live with the abuse anymore. I couldn't live wondering when you might quit punching yourself and punch me. I couldn't wonder anymore if...*

I stop myself and take my thoughts captive as the mediator begins. A man in his fifties. Dressed in simple formal attire. A cross on the back wall of this office adorned by pictures of school-age children. The point of this meeting is to come to some agreement, some form of terms in the possibility that we might avoid trial in this divorce. That by some good graces we can pretend to like each other enough for thirty seconds to both say yes about something, sign on the dotted line, walk away free from each other forever, and forget all of this ever happened. At least, that's the world's view of divorce. The view that says, *"Why can't we be divorced? Because God says we can't? Well screw that."* Those words, they're real to me. They hurt.

Mediator begins. Over three grueling hours, he asked me questions about sharing our children, how we could, why I feel the way

I feel, what aspects are most important to me in their raising. And you know what, friend? It was hard. It could be so much easier to say, sure, I will let them go to church wherever, go to school wherever, do this and that and not fight for them.

But no. God gifted my daughters to me. In that gifting, He entrusted their souls and the shepherding of them into my care. I am the ambassador to my daughters first before anything else. Responsibility to guide them into an eternal relationship with our heavenly Father and teach them to love Him; that is my first goal in this life now. I believe it was Andy Stanley who said, "It might not be what you do for the kingdom, but who you raise."

I had to stand firm in that conviction even when my attorney was saying, "Is religion that big of a deal? Is Christian schooling really *that* important when you live in such a great public school district?" (All of this is my story, friends. It might resonate with you, and it might be so far from your story and your heartbreak. But listen. God is in the details.)

Three grueling hours passed. Questions lingered back and forth. Every word in my ear, "Let your reasonableness be made known to all men. The Lord is near. Reasonableness. Mackenzie. Be reasonable." I can still hear it resounding in every fiber of my nerves to this day. I'll spare you the details of the whitewash that I believed was that mediation. Near the end, the mediator was obviously flustered. He had no resolve. No answers, no justification. He turned to my then husband as he continued to berate me with attitude.

And as clear as the blue skies over Montana, the words, "Mackenzie is as reasonable as a person can be. She is offering everything she can here. She is reasonable. You are not."

My heart pounded so loudly I'm sure it nearly dropped to the first floor. Did you catch that? God gave me that exact word over three hours prior as I sought him in that hallway. Reasonable. Present. The LORD was present. In every minute of my battle, there He was. Showing up to fight. But that wasn't all. No. That was just a part of this story.

We discussed details of every aspect as every marriage dissolving must. But the only troublesome spot for me was giving up the right to my daughters' education. He wanted full rights. Many would argue that he is the father and would (of course) maintain or deserve a say. In my state, it's nearly impossible for one parent to maintain all of the rights for children. So fighting over details seemed monotonous, I'm quite sure, to the court system.

Friends, please don't miss my point here. You don't know the details of my whole story, nor do I want to release that here. However, I would be remiss and understating God's glory if some of these moments were swept away and untold forever. Remember, God told me to write these. They are moments that can be used to encourage you so that even in your darkest hour or scariest moments, you are without a doubt never too far from the tangible presence of grace.

So what did I do? I fought for their education. Without too much of a history lesson, I'll give you the dummies' update on my educational history. As a child, I attended a tiny, private Christian school. Very conservative, highly educational. My best friends are sisters I gained from that experience. My high school education was nontraditional as a homeschooler. We were snowbirds, living in both Florida and Ohio during those formative years. It was an experience I hold dear to my heart, often convinced that homeschooling would be the perfect choice for my future children just as it was for me.

I attended a local secular university and graduated at the top of my class with both awards and honors before entering into the field of education, where I then taught public elementary school during the day and privately tutored on evenings and weekends. It was not long before I was married and expecting my first daughter, which is when we chose together that I would have the honor of being a stay-at-home mom. If you were to know me, you would know that being called *wife and mother* are the greatest desires that God has laid within the corners of my heart as He wove me together. Nothing made my heart happier than having a family to attend to. It was my servitude. It was my joy and peace and fulfillment. Oh, how I ache as I lack part of that identity now.

Nonetheless, I tell you all of this for what happens next in my story. Never in the course of this life did I recognize the steps that I was taking had already been laid out for me. In fact, I had a longing to study many other paths in college but chose education first. I never really knew why. I love children and learning. It seemed fitting. But it was never my burning passion in total honesty. (So sorry to any of my professors. I loved so many of you. But it's just the truth.) When the mediator began digging deeper into the education aspects, he wanted to know why I was so keen on the idea of either homeschooling or Christian education.

Honestly, the words came out jumbled and confusing as I stated how I want my daughters to have a foundation of faith. He understood but asked why we couldn't just be involved in church. (We were.) I stumbled more. It wasn't long before my then husband jumped on the bandwagon. It felt like an attack. But I had to make a stand, make a plea for what calling was in my heart. He started attacking the idea of private school, attempting to make a mockery of me, belittling me as a homeschooler and product of private education. Someone who lives in a *bubble* and *doesn't understand the real world because I was just homeschooled.*

I stood firm. Reasonable. Never indulging in immature conduct. Without hesitation, the mediator took a sip of his coffee mug. I noticed the Bible verse inscribed across the front. He glanced at me. He then sat the cup down in front of us before stating, "My children went to private Christian school." (Insert mic drop here.)

Are you listening, friends? Are you hearing God's work and details and words omnipresent in my story? Is He not just the most amazing being? To God be the glory! *To God be the glory.*

Less than forty-eight hours passed and two days before Christmas, we returned to that same hallway. Except instead of being inside the room, the same three hours were spent in that forsaken hallway as our attorneys battled back and forth. My attorney assured me this was not over. It would get worse before it would get better. We had a long road to go after an already longer year behind us.

Several times our legal counsel came out to discuss issues privately. That last issue though? Still hanging heavily in the polluted air. My counsel wanted to know if I would give the girls' father the rights and choices to their education. I could have everything else. But that was the one issue that burned within me so strongly.

"No. I can't." My attorney looked at me with crazy eyes.

"You do realize this could go to trial? You do realize you are fighting over school? I've never had this happen in forty years of practicing law!" he said as he was obviously irritated with me.

I could sense the frustration in his tone. I looked at him as a once timid young woman and found some gusto buried deep within my weary soul.

"Sir, I attended private Christian schooling until eighth grade. I was then homeschooled. I graduated from a secular university at the top of my class with awards and honors before working in the public school system as an educator. I have a hand and foot in quite literally every single facet of education. So. No, sir. There is no one on this earth more qualified to make my children's educational decisions than me. I am convicted and will refuse with all of my being to give up that right."

He looked at me half-astonished. Having had no idea about my educational background, I'm pretty sure he smirked at me. Almost proud. He sauntered back to the private room.

I walked out of that courthouse that day with hope in my heart. I had gained full custody of my daughters. Even educational rights. It was all over. Everything I had never wanted. Done. And then? The tears came.

I cried. All day. All night. But I didn't just cry for the pain and the feeling of death that lingered in my heart. Many of the tears came when I realized with pure certainty that all along, the years that I spent in college changing majors, the schools I worked at after graduation, the choices my parents made to send me to Christian school and homeschool me, every single step of my life was directed and ordained by God. None of that made any sense to me until that day. That moment in that hallway. If every moment of my educational experiences was for this battle alone, for the season of war to engage the enemy and say, "No, you don't get the final say!" then it was all worth it. Every. Single. Step. God's within every detail of our lives, friends. Even when we don't see it happening.

Proverbs 16: 9 states, "A man's heart plans his way, but the Lord directs his steps."

I tell you all of this with a little bit of fear. Fear of judgment. Of naysayers. The vulnerability that comes with opening the book of your life and asking people to look inside. But more than anything, I choose to be cautious with the details of my divorce for the benefit of the kingdom. You see, friend, I do believe that marriages can overcome. Marriages face trials and affairs and addictions and overcome. And sometimes marriages face mental health issues and abuse and don't overcome. At the end of the day, we are two imperfect beings who chose to come together in a very broken world.

Divorce should never be the first choice. It should never be an easy out. It is the worst thing to happen to me in my life, and the worst part is, this happened to my children. The details I have chosen to hide on a shelf are for me and God. (And my therapist.) If I choose to share them with the world, I fear women will use them for themselves in order to validate their personal experiences. And furthermore, although I am no longer in love with that man, I will choose daily to love him as Christ calls me to love him, even if often he feels like my enemy. He is still a soul. God is still seeking Him. And As Bob Goff would remind me, it is, after all, "*the difficult people that are the hardest to love*" (*Everybody Always*).

Love takes on many forms. It is possible to love, pray for, and still be at war with the other side. I may never have had to take the stand in that courtroom, but sister, we are still on trial for the Lord. We have an audience watching our every move. Be aware that the words you speak, the actions you take, and the demeanor you carry may be the only representation of the gospel of Christ that people see. Our response to our circumstances is a direct reflection of Christ and a testimony to His kingdom.

Wield your sword wisely. The world is watching.

9

Future

The future is so uncertain to us. Stop me if I'm wrong here, but I look around and see so many women today racing to overcome (or faking the achievement) the death that is divorce. They're powerful and united and *running the world*. I see them move on with new men, sometimes back to their ex, not taking any of this seriously. They're running from fling to fling, arm to arm, bed to bed, searching for something. Anything to complete them. Searching to be happy, longing for acceptance, validation, and of course the obvious, love. But at what cost?

Often, they marry more quickly than they did possibly the first time. The desire within us is innate though. That yearning, knitted within our souls to union with a person—my person, that person, any person—someone who truly knows you and wants you. The struggle has never been so real, my friends. I'm not pointing judgmental fingers here at the women who are walking this path. I know firsthand how awful the feeling of being alone day after day can be. It's different when your single friends welcome you back. If they've never experienced marriage, chances are they haven't experienced this level of loneliness. They mean well, but it just isn't the same. The reality is: no man can or will ever increase your worth or value. How can they? You are already a daughter of the King.

I'm going to dive into the dark precipice that is my soul right now. Jump into that ugly side of single and the overwhelming of lonely. The reality of what some days hold and reminder that in acceptance, it is okay to grieve. It's okay to be a little lost and beaten down, just as long as we don't remain there in that darkness. Angst and frustration are traits that like to remind me from time to time that *"I'm not good enough and probably never will be."*

When the depression seeps in or crashes upon you, remember whose voice still controls the waves. Remember that the darkness runs and hides at the sound of our Father, and in His light no darkness can dare remain. Remember John 1:5? *"The light shines in the darkness, and the darkness has not overcome it."*

I have a charge for you: on the hardest days, hours, moments, choose the person that you want to be. Who is she? What does she look like? (Not in a physical sense but more mentally/spiritually.) What attributes does she emulate to those around her? I know I see a woman full of compassion, grace, servitude. I want to be more like her. Chase after her. Catch her. And with consistency, pass her with the expectation of what might be waiting up ahead for you. Rejoicing in hope is what Christ wants for us.

Searching for new life and a new normal is not bad. In fact, it can be healthy in moderation. Something I've learned in the last few years is that it is okay to find a healthy hobby and enjoy the time for yourself doing it. For me, Holy Yoga opened doors and taught me the art of meditation with Christ. It has allowed me to learn how to worship with my exercise, breathe my life back to my Creator, and taught me such vulnerability is often the only key to true acceptance of our circumstance. Golf has also been something I have enjoyed in my few spare hours of free time. It's a sport that forces my mental capacity to quiet itself in order to obtain certain goals. (Oddly enough, golf would serve as a catalyst later in my story that would bring me exciting, new adventures and friends. You just never know how God is working behind the scenes.)

I enjoy the calmness and the posture of a slow course. Honestly, I could (okay *usually)* play terribly but that's not the point here. I love to talk to God when I'm focusing on that little ball. He reminds me that while the whole world around me is still spinning on its axis and rotating wildly out of control, right now, in this quiet moment, He's here. He's calm. Collected. Quiet. And at peace—always.

What a reminder of the peace that I long for in my life. I want to chase after that feeling (okay, maybe that golf ball)! I want to see where I can take it. Sometimes it's deep into the woods and a total mistake, and other times it's a perfect shot with consistent practice. Nevertheless, it's in the moving forward, in the motion of it all, the bravery to move, that's where the growth happens.

I challenge you. Find an activity, even if it's something you can do at home that will bring you a sliver of joy and honor God in how you perform it. He will fulfill you in whatever way you choose. Don't wait to find something. Is it writing? Journaling? Blogging? Playing an instrument? Maybe cooking or baking? Crocheting or even reading a book in the quiet hours? Find a rhythm for your desires, organize a few minutes to accomplish them, and maintain that. Seek it. Pray for God to honor it. And before you know it, you will watch your lonely hours dissipate into the night just as the fading moon changes places with the rising dawn.

Do you want to know my heart condition? What a vulnerable place this is for me to share with you, friend. A place where there are scars from deep wounds like that ugly vision I depicted a while back. Also darkness because after all, I, too, am human. Joy because Christ dwells within. But so does doubt.

Even though my divorce is long over, the court dates are finished, the papers signed and sealed away, I'm still always humbled by the transparency that aches deep within my heart. God has often given me the desires I have asked for. He gave me a husband. He did not promise me forever with him. God walked through the furnace with me in a custody battle, and as much as my daughters were initially a gift from heaven for this time, He also gave me my daughters a second time to raise and train up in His admonition. I choose to believe that the desires of my heart were placed within me by my Creator when He knitted me together. He gave me and you the longing for companionship and friendship.

This kind of desire is grounded in the theology of woman being taken from man and formed as a part of her very own flesh and bone, who was later breathed new life into from the sovereignty of the one and only Almighty. A longing to serve my family in a way that I struggle to verbalize. A desire within me to be a wife burning and aching so, that the tears streaming down my face when I pour my heart on the altar of grace are only lightened by the reminder that He knows. He knows because He put that in me. All of it. The longing, the aching and burning and desire and friendship and servitude and even the very last droplet of tears. He formed those traits in me, and whatever the innate desires you think you've hidden deep inside? He placed those within you too.

The words that I was once called here on earth are not the names that my Father named me from the second I was formed. Have you ever considered what He named you? Someday in heaven, we will be called by the name that He chose for us long ago. To hear His voice speak love and acceptance in our forever home will cover and erase the painful words we have endured on earth. But for now, I choose to remember the names I know He calls us. Chosen.

Doesn't it feel amazing to know that even though we often run so far from grace, He is still standing there waiting? I like to picture a father on his front porch with some sweet tea and a smile just waiting for his kids to come home from a long day of playing in the fields. He's standing there smiling, calling us *chosen.* He's calling us love. *Love.*

He created us and saw our weakness and sin nature and failures and shame. *Still* says we are His love. Redeemed because He didn't have to give us murderers His only perfect, beautiful child, but He did. Just because He wants us. Not because He needs us. I could go on for days, but sister, those names were given to you by the highest authority. It only seems fitting that we wear those titles with acceptance and gratitude and sprinkle in some joy like confetti because sometimes you just have to laugh to keep from crying!

I don't know what the future holds for you or me. But as many wise folks before me have said, I do know who holds my future. Often there's this annoying little chirping noise on my shoulder from the evil one. On the days when I give in and listen, I hear these words, "You aren't enough. You're a single, divorced Christian woman. Who would want *you*? What kind of nice Christian guy is looking for a girl like you with baggage and scars? Who do you think you are? What will a nice guy's family have to say about your circumstances? How can you even think anyone will want you again?"

So ugly, am I right? My tears burn my eyes as I write those words. They cut into the deepest part of my heart. I hate my labels. I hate that often I let them define me instead of the labels God has spoken for me. So today, I choose to leave them right here on this page. They won't leave the screen when I close this down. They won't follow me to my bedroom as I lay in my bed. They won't wake with me as I hit my snooze button tomorrow morning more times than I care to admit. And even if they try to sneak up on me in the days ahead, I'll replace them with truths such as chosen, love, and redeemed.

What words are you hearing whispered at you, sister? Lies that you cannot escape that feel so true you want to erase them forever from your vocabulary? Quiet. Let's lay them down at the altar together tonight and leave them. Grace has better names for you. Let's walk out of the shame together. Onward. Upward. Into the future, warrior woman.

10

Nothing Is Unseen

Have you ever experienced a protection so profound, so deep, and so vast that it shakes you to your core? In a world where we live in a state of perpetual fear, hate, division, racism, anguish, abuse, scandals, disappointment, and betrayal, it's hard to verbalize the profound protection that our Father in heaven is bestowing on our daily lives, down to the wire, moment, even second. Sometimes it's hard to recognize it's happening at all.

Recently, I had an experience, an opportunity that was essentially years in the making, one I had asked Christ for in the quiet moments. It was really reaching out there. I won't share all the details because they don't much matter here in the mortal moments, but trust me when I say it was a "God, should I even be asking for this *really* rather silly thing? Should I do this?" A ridiculous kind of prayer.

I spent two weeks of seeking God in prayer before I sent someone a simple message. And you know what? That two weeks of consistent obedience and vulnerability opened doors and friendships and experiences for me that never would otherwise have been opened in my life. Nearly three months passed and I had forgotten this request I made. But you see, God hadn't forgotten that desire in my heart even though I had. And can you guess what He did? He granted it.

Three more grueling months passed before I nearly had an answer to that same silly question. Basically, I got some quiet time with a super fun person in the field of Christianity whom I greatly enjoy and admire. A man who loves Jesus. A man who has human struggles and fears and failures. A man who places his career on the line every single day for the sake of vulnerability and risk-taking all in the name of Jesus. All for the message of hope that lies within the local church.

Don't get too excited here; the importance of this is in the uncertainty and the quiet. And it will remain there. It wasn't until I made this new friend and had the sweetest little adventure with him that I sat at home in the quiet and poured my thankful heart back to God with gratitude and thanksgiving that I realized God's presence in the tiny details of it all.

This little weekend adventure of mine was nothing more than a planned date ahead of time to visit family out of town. A weekend to rest. As it had turned out, my cousin's boyfriend had to pass on an opportunity to visit her, so the chance for a mini girl's vacation became all mine. And I took it. Little did I know this would all unravel together from that one request I had made to God into a woven story all tied together with a bright red bow in the cold courses of a November day. A story that had only the most magnificent Creator's hand writing on it.

It was November. It had rained for a solid week and was downright freezing. Northeast. (Hard pass on this weather up here, you guys.) My dad asked me if I had checked the oil in my car, as all great dads do. His way of exhibiting love. He reminded me that there was *no way* I would be golfing this weekend per my scheduled plans. As we hugged goodbye and I headed out of town, the roads were obviously wet, cars were flying past me. I'm a good driver. Not tooting my own horn here, guys, but in my midthirties I've never even had a speeding ticket. *Yet.*

I was uneasy but prepared for a great weekend and excited to get to my destination. I headed out of town and made it only one-fourth of the way to my destination before the misty rain turned to torrential downpour. In an instant, everything changed. Two cars ahead of me, I see collision. One car turns sideways. The car in front of me T-bones the first car. Debris flying. I see brake lights in the rain. Two more cars slip into the accident and before I know it, all I see is an eighteen-wheeler in my rearview mirror barreling down on me at breakneck speed.

Without hesitation, I heard both my heavenly Father and my dad in my head saying, *"Don't panic."* It all happened so fast. With white knuckles, I shouted, "Okay, Jesus! Let's do this." (There was definite fear in my voice, but I can admit it's funnier now.)

I assumed at the very least I would clip one of the cars' fenders. I wove right, then left, then skidded over to an exit. Unscathed. Untouched. No damage to me. Physically anyway.

I watched the eighteen-wheeler crawl out of the accident as I frantically called 911. To this day I have no answer how I made it out of that accident without as much as a scratch on my car. God's hand of protection; His army of angels were surrounding me in that terrifying moment and glided me and my car directly through that massive accident. He was teaching me. Again. *"I've got this."*

I take these moments and often say, "Remember when…" God was in that moment and He protected me and it was a miracle and so cool, but then I turn around when things don't continue in my way and wonder where His hand of protection was then.

"Well, why did God let my husband treat me that way? Why couldn't He save my marriage? Where was He when I was crying myself to sleep every night? Where was He when I couldn't make my husband stop?"

Do you do this too? I think it's so much our flawed humanity really. Even those of us who seek God out daily, who strive to be more like Jesus and love Him and serve him, we have to recognize that no matter how *Christian* we are, we are still merely human. There is no part of me that will ever be as perfect, beautiful, servant-hearted, flat-out good as Jesus Christ. This is where we realize how our only option is to bow at the foot of the throne, bring all of our brokenness, our shame, our guilt, our vulnerability, and say, *"Here I am, God, choose me."*

And you know what? He will. Because God doesn't want us only when we're perfect and in a good place in a healthy state of mind. He wants us with our heart's sickness and our sin nature and our evil tendencies and our shame of being an addict or an abuser or the abused or the adulterer.

Don't let your humanity be the only thing that stops you from wholly seeking Christ's heart. He created you. He knows all of you already. Even the darkest parts, and there's nothing you can do to stop Him from loving you.

I have a bad habit of saying, "Look what God did over here and how He rescued me right there in that moment of my life," and then turning around when I'm sad and hurt and forgetting those tangible moments where He allowed me the opportunity to see His protection are only (if I had to guess) the tip of the iceberg. The more I think of it, He's always working behind the scenes to make provisions for me, to make all the pieces fall into place right where He intends them to fall. *Annnnd* here's the crappy, hard part. It's all in His timing—*not mine.* Boom. That's the hard part, right? *But I want it now!*

In this story I'm only briefly retelling you, that's what happened to me. Months went by. I had actually forgotten my initial request I sent. God didn't forget; He just said, *"Hey, girl, in my time."* But when I had no idea He was even working for my behalf, He was. He was planting my steps in accordance with His will and plan when I was busy in the mundane routine of life. And I believe that in the quiet moments of my obedience, even in my sadness, loneliness, moments of healing, He was, all along, preparing this gift for me. A moment of happiness and joy that only He would understand because He is the only one who sees inside the far corners of my heart, and only He would see the joy that came from giving His daughter this gift. That's just like our heavenly Father; sometimes we forget He sees us as His children. He desires to see us joyful, and He still delights in the moments that make our hearts happy when they align perfectly with His will for us.

I choose not to bore you with the details of my request and for a little bit of fear in sounding like a crazy woman. (And also out of respect for this other person's privacy.) God took my initial question from six months earlier, wrapped them in a neatly tied bow, and handed them to me on a beautiful golf course in eastern Michigan on a freezing, cold November morning. He gave me the courage to go out of my comfort zones, to ask for something I never would have dreamed, and to show up and be present without social media or cell phones or expectations for that matter.

The best part was? We golfed. (Pretty terribly actually.) And we joked, and we rode around that bitter cold golf course until our faces were numb and our hands didn't wrap around our clubs properly anymore. We lost more golf balls than I can recall, and after it was all over, I had simply made a new friend. And God saw the joy that an answered prayer had made me, and He was pleased.

I spent some time that weekend making new friends, visiting old friends, laughing until the tears flowed, enjoying the autumn leaves over the highways and the beautiful cascading views of a USGA-ranked golf course. God finished my special weekend with more gifts than I could have ever asked for. The kinds that change hearts and mend brokenness and bind souls together forever.

I left Michigan looking up to the sky proclaiming God's goodness. Knowing that even if I didn't get everything I wanted all the time, He still gave me exactly what I had asked for in my uncertainty and then sprinkled a little more joy on top of that! More joy than even I could have ever imagined.

When I finally made it home, I was greeted with a card from my aunt. I recall standing in the doorway at my parent's house in Northeast Ohio in tears, reflecting over the past weekend with my mom. Recanting with her of how genuinely loved I felt by our Creator. How He took something so tiny in the grand scheme of this overwhelming world, a request I hadn't made known to anyone but Him, and granted it.

I opened the card to find a gift, but the gift wasn't tangible. No. Her words were the gift of peace that my heart needed to hear. Words that took moments from my childhood, teen years, and my broken adulthood and gathered them together into one profound phrase. *A phrase that would later title this book.* A phrase that would acknowledge God's consistent presence in my life. A confirmation of what was happening with these words that I am writing to you.

Words. They hold such power to tear us down, but don't they also have such strength to build us up?

Here's where I want you to listen, really listen, sister. I don't know what deep, hidden desires you lock inside your heart. Maybe right now, they're just to make it out of the court system alive or unscathed at best. Maybe you're just making it paycheck to paycheck and waiting for a financial break. Maybe you're past this and like me, with a heart that's healing in restoration and ready to turn the page or start a new chapter, you're always a little afraid to ask God for something more. Don't be afraid to ask God. Don't be afraid to fall on your knees ever. No matter how big. How small. How intimate. Ask God to give you the grace and courage for whatever it is you're asking of Him. We honor Him with the magnitudes of our requests.

It might not happen. It might take ten years to happen. It might take six months to happen. And like me, you might even forget you asked for it in the first place. But the important thing to take away from here is, if I can ask for the simple gift of golf in a special place with a random person and He expounds on it, multiplies the blessing, and makes it known for no other reason than to make His presence visible and tangible to me, then He can do the exact same thing for you. And God wants to show up for you and He is showing up for you and He will continue to show up for you.

The most beautiful part of this story for me, though, is how God worked in my waiting. I had no idea He was preparing such a sweet gift for me. I trusted in the quiet moments, found hope that He is still good even when it seems impossible to find goodness. He took laughter, the best medicine *("A merry heart is a good medicine" (Proverbs 17:22))*, and used it as a salve to medicate my wounds. And eventually, that exact same joy was the same agent that brought my story altogether under one roof. Even when we can't see it, He is always showing up in the waiting.

In my story, it took six months of waiting. But the truth is, my story isn't over yet. The waiting isn't over either. Not even close. God is still up there working and writing my story and yours. I can't wait for the future! To look back one day and say, "Oh, wow, God! I see what you were doing now! That's so cool!"

Trust me, sister. It's *so* worth the wait. Make your requests known, hide nothing from Him, and then the hard part—wait upon the Lord. For He is good. So good.

Sometimes our prayers are unanswered. We live in a world of instant gratification. Our fingertips can give us anything we want right away without repentance. It makes it so hard for us in this day to actually be patient and wait. We want to make things happen in our own timing; why wait on God when we can make it happen right now? But something else I need to remind you of is, in that waiting, God might also be protecting us from something harmful. Because just like I asked for something trivial, and although I got it, I immediately wanted more. And then when I didn't get it, I was sad.

That's the heart for you. Turns on you in an instant. It's in these moments, the *no* moments, the wait moments, the hard moments, we have to remember that although we think we know what might be best for us right now or the future, that we serve a sovereign God who knows our future better than we do. He knows if that request we want is not for our best interest. He knows if the people we want to bring into our lives postdivorce are healthy, accepting, or right for us.

So what do we do? We humbly seek His face. And in the trials of waiting, which goodness I know is a pain, I also know from this past experience how prevalent God was in the waiting. Even when I had no idea He was working, He was formulating the puzzle pieces of that weekend to all fall together. The weekend that I wasn't initially invited to. The golf course I had wanted to try out, I was asked to be a guest at. The home I had never visited was opened with hospitality. New friends and family were made. New memories, now old, still not forgotten, and all for the simple reason that I once bowed down on my knees in the shower (my prayer closet; don't judge me), lifted my hands, and asked God for. One. Simple. Gift.

And guess what? He heard me. And He hears you. And He sees your tears. And He laughs when you smile. And His heart skips a beat when you find joy again. This is our *good, good Father* who chooses only to prosper you. Step out now, girl, from the pain and the anguish, and when you're ready, choose to turn the page. Ask our Father to grant your deepest desires, but only when they align with

His. Ask Him to show you His will for your life. To guide you on the path of righteousness for His name's sake. To give you the desire to seek His will above all else.

And if you continue in this, abiding in His will, these quiet moments of begging God for wisdom, discernment, to change your heart to be more like His, to make your life look more like Jesus, I promise. One day you, too, will look back. And you will see the trail of neatly tied little bows all adorned with the Savior's signature. Reminding you that He has been here all along, never leaving you, never forsaking you, and proving to you over and over again that *you* are a chosen daughter of the Most High King, and just how profoundly loved by Him you truly are.

11

Live Wire

The following is an excerpt from a personal journal entry. This experience exists in my life for no other reason than to prove God's sovereignty. In an instant, He proved yet again to me that my prayers are heard. That even the smallest details of our lives matter to His heart, and sometimes, all we have to do is ask.

It had just nearly passed 7:00 a.m., and I crawled out of bed. Anxiety weighed heavy on my chest and shoulders. My head was pounding from lack of sleep. Today feels different.

Two minutes pass and I realize I still have to make the coffee, dang. Forgot to set it up the night before. Quietly I tiptoe to the couch for a little quiet time with God.

Today I have to share my girls with their father. Normal in the course of these tragedies. It's for five whole days this time. The most ever. To most moms, five days would be a vacation. A break, a chance to sleep. But when sharing time with your babies is a by-product and detriment of divorce, it's different.

A year ago, a few hours without my girls in my realm of vision would've sent me into a panic attack. Some (okay, my therapist) might've called it survival mode. I'm thankful that nearly a year later, some great therapy and lots and lots of prayer, I finally came to realize that those panic-riddled thoughts are yet another tactic the evil one uses to distract and destroy the peace of mind that God wants to provide in an attempt to destroy the harmony I can find only with Him.

7:05

I beg God to provide me with only a few extra hours with my babies. "Lord, I know I have to share your children today with their father. My heart is so heavy. My chest hurts." My eyes well with tears. "Please, Father, I don't know what you can do, but I have faith that you are capable to stall the morning." I complete my prayers with, "Father, please grant me a few extra hours with my girls today. I trust you to guard them. They are yours first. Amen."

What happened next some would call pure coincidence. Not me. I call it God incidence.

7:20

Through tearstained eyes, I see little warm red faces pop around the corner. "Mommy?" I take in the melody of those words. We snuggle under cozy blankets by the fire as we recall their silly nighttime dreams.

7:45

I receive a text from a friend across the main street. "What is happening on your road?" I peer out my windows but can only catch a glimpse of flashing lights. Still in my bathrobe, I throw on my winter hat and coat, fuzzy slippers, and drudge down my driveway in the winter wind and rain to the sidewalk. What a sight to see! (Me, not the commotion.) As it turns out, the only entrance and exit to our development is barricaded by fire trucks, police cars, and yellow barrels all surrounded by orange cones. Lots of men stand around. (Some probably wondering who that crazy lady in her bathrobe is.) The main road had been shut down. No time frame for when it will reopen.

A live wire has fallen directly across my street. No cars will be permitted to enter or exit until further notice.

8:00 a.m.

I look up to the heavens. The rain is hitting my face, the wind is blowing my hat off. But all I can do is laugh. I laugh at the understanding of *my Father*. I laugh for *joy* that I get to have a few extra hours with my daughters. He heard my words. He felt my pain. He recognized my faith. He answered my simple prayer.

God is just like that, isn't He? A live wire smack-dab right in the intersection of our lives. Demanding that we recognize His presence. Sometimes it takes a storm and pain for us to see, but He is right here in the middle of everything making His presence known. And on top of it all, I think He likes to remind us that He has a pretty good sense of humor about it all too.

As Christians in this all too fast-paced and progressive society, I believe it's easy for us to forget that God is still very much working all around us, within us, in ways that we can still see his handiwork. Why is this so hard for us to recognize? We're told that He is *"the same yesterday, today, forever"* (Hebrews 13:8). So what makes us believe that the same God who literally parted the Red Sea and turned goblets of water into wine in miraculous, physical form is not still the exact same God who dwells within the very realms of our world with us even so right now? He is just as able and willing to perform miracles for you and me as He was for the Israelites. Let's not diminish the capacity of what He can do for our lives. Which lends me to my humbly asking of Him, "Beauty for ashes, God? I want beauty for *my* ashes, please?"

I know deep down God is capable of giving me everything I could ever desire in accordance with His will. I know there is no mountain too high for Him. But my humanity reminds me of this little thing called realism. Ever heard of it? It stops me in my tracks every time. That side of life that says, *"Well I also asked God to save my marriage, and He didn't do that, so why would He do this thing for me now?"* I don't know that answer, sister. But I sure have walked that road right alongside you.

What I do know for certain is that deep down inside the crevices of my cracked heart, God has planted something inside of me. A seed that is to take this brokenness, my vulnerability and pain, and bury it. To make something so terrible and unbearable that I can't even stand the thought of and use it for His glory and goodness. The harsh truth is, often we cannot become refined until we've been through a fire. We can't grow a garden without the toil of pushing through the soil first.

When my friend's house burned down in the middle of winter two years ago, he stood in church in front of me, the elders, and others as we consoled them. He looked at us as he held his wife and five beautiful children and said, "Now, we rebuild…because after all, we can't have a testimony without a test."

Guys. That shook me to my core. He had decided right then and there, with nothing but a family of seven to provide for, the clothes on their back, and God on their side, that this would only make them stronger. That they would rise from the literal ashes of a nightmare house fire just weeks before Christmas and begin again.

Don't you see it? God can take all of these things that you and I have lived—these tests, the grief—plant them in the ashes of our wounds and the remnants of the fire that is a failed marriage, and bury them deep in the embers of our hearts.

Sister, have you ever buried anything in ashes before? No? Well, this pretty magical thing happens when you do. Ashes act as a compost in soil. They actually irrigate it, nurture it with nutrients, and promote a pretty insane ground for growth. If you don't believe me, try it sometime. But the amazing part here is what comes out of the ashes.

A while back we had a tree stump. A pretty rough and ugly thing that refused to be ground down. So what did we do? We burned it. Ashes remained. And eventually we planted some sunflowers in the leftover ugly albeit fertile ground, unaware of what would happen next. Flourishing. That's what happened next. Those flowers grew taller and faster and bigger and brighter than any flower I had ever planted before. (And let me tell you, I *love* to garden.) Those flowers were strong enough to withhold any summer gale and rooted deep enough to harbor the toughest of rains. Kids ran them over with motorized toys, birds ate from them…do you see the moral here? If not for the fire, for the ashes that remained from that ugly thing in my yard, no flowers would have flourished. No future feeding ground would have emerged, no beauty for the eye to behold would have been witnessed.

And the very same thing is happening right here with you. Right now, in the fire, in the heat, in the sulfur, every time you choose Christ first, every time you run to Him with your pain and confusion and setbacks, something is happening in the quiet. A seed. A planting. Deep within you. Do you feel it? The ashes are only a substitute, a conduit, for what can emerge. Beauty for ashes. Let's not just be the girls who say that. Let's be the girls who believe it. And then, let's prove it.

For I believe that out of the ashes can come a great and fierce awakening.

12

Provision

I have but one more Lifetime-esque story to share with you that is without a doubt a tangible representation of the hand of God working in my life. Remember, I'm not telling you these God moments to make you question, "Why doesn't God speak to me this way? Why aren't these things happening for me?" But aren't they, sister? I think that if we are aligning ourselves in the heart of Jesus and following him in faithful obedience, He simply allows us the grace enough to see a little more clearly the tasks and gifts that He has for us. I am no more ordained to receive love and gifts and grace from our God than you.

In fact, I bet if you start looking for God in the daily, you will see many moments where He really is showing up to bat for you more often than you realize. We all have our blinders on. We choose to believe in karma and good luck and fallacies far more than the facts of a gracious God and Father who really wants us to receive His bounty. Start looking for it. Start thanking Him for the little moments. And soon your heart's posture will change to an attitude of gratitude.

I was thick in the drudges of my divorce at this particular point in my life. My soon-to-be ex-husband believed we would get back together and was waiting on me to stop *playing house* and wondering when I would stop *"being a strong independent woman"* (his words not mine) as I prepared to move my girls and I into our first home as a single woman and mother. I had nothing. Barely a job, no money, no child support, no credit, but I knew this was the next right thing. And also the hardest thing.

I was still housekeeping as a side job to earn some extra money outside of my office work. On this particular day, my heart was flooded with despair. I managed to make one right choice and decided to listen to some worship music. I vacuumed. I mopped. I worshipped. I cried. Choices like those seem trivial, simply choosing one genre of music over another, but I do believe they are the little moments that will ultimately affect our personalities and either build us up inside or tear us down. The old adage, what goes in, comes out, has never been truer.

Tired in every form, I sat down to rest and have a quick lunch. To this day I recall what chair I sat on, what clothes I had on, and the weak mood of my heart. I opened my phone browser and started jotting down what immediate items I would need for our new home. Now if you were to know me at all, you would know that cleaning is part of my DNA. It's no mistake that God ordained me to finding housekeeping jobs long before my marital separation. I *love* to clean and organize. It's so weird, I know.

Naturally, like any good OCD person, the first item on my list was a sweeper. Okay. I google vacuums—the brand I prefer—and start searching. After ten minutes, I had settled on one that I knew I could manage to work for and afford within a week's pay and time frame. But then, like a load of bricks, it hit me. *What am I doing? I can't even afford a stinking sweeper. Let alone the paint and tools and furniture I need to supply my girls with a real home. How can I even do this, Lord? I literally have nothing!*

And just like that, the tears began to flow. I poured my heart out to Christ like a spoiled child begging for something on Christmas that I really didn't deserve. I cried as I told him how broken I felt, how abandoned I was, and how I'm literally thirty years old and starting over from scratch.

He listened. I looked at the vacuum one more time on my phone. Decided I would give all of my uncertainty to God and stopped my self-loathing long enough to moan this prayer, *"Jesus, you know what I need before I ever needed it. You know what the sparrow needs. You know the number of hairs on my head. I trust that you see me, and I trust you will provide exactly what I need in your timing, not my own. Please, help me to get through this, Father."*

And just like that, I turned my music back on, and with a gentler spirit, I went back to my job of being housekeeper for the day. Not one other soul on this planet knew my desire. Not one other person heard or saw my tears. Just Jesus. Completely Jesus. And what happened next will forever be a transformative moment for me in my life.

I finished the cleaning job and hurried home to get my daughters before another busy evening of activities and chores. I poured my exhausted self onto my mom's porch where a large box was sitting. *Wonder what that is?* I thought to myself. *Rather large for an Amazon delivery.*

I shrugged it off and settled into the kitchen where my toddler was waiting with a snack. A minute later, my mother emerged from the hallway in high spirits.

"Hi, honey! How was work? We had a great day here. What's the plan for this evening?" The usual chitchat. Very cheerful. My mother is a saint in human form. She would constantly maintain a cheerful countenance to keep me from bursting into tears at any given moment.

"Fine," I answered. Trying to remember how to be cautiously cheerful in my own words; tending to my little ones' needs while hiding my own weary smile.

She turned around and said, *"Oh! Well, guess what? We went to Sam's Club today!"*

Okay, I thought. *Great, groceries.* (Guess again.)

She continued, *"You know that little clearance section they have? They had the most perfect sweeper for you! Only one left! We picked it up for you because I thought you might need one for your new home."*

My jaw fell to the floor. I ran to the porch and turned the box on its side to see the picture. And there it was. In all its glory, *the* sweeper. Not just any sweeper. *The exact, same sweeper.* The same brand, the same color, the same shape and size that only mere hours before I had sat at a lonely dining room table crying over. The very same sweeper that brought me to tears over not being able to provide for myself and my girls. The same sweeper that only Jesus knew was in my heart, and not one other person on this planet had been there for.

I couldn't verbalize my emotions. Stunned, I turned to my mom and began weeping just as my poor sister-in-law walked in on this very confusing dialogue.

"What the heck was going on here? Crying over a purple sweeper?" (Her face said it all. If she didn't already think I was a little cray cray, this surely solidified it for her.)

My mother was just as confused as I stumbled over the words to explain what had just happened. "That sweeper. I wanted it. Only God knew. How did you…?"

I'll spare you the next few hours of babbling to actually get the story out enough for everyone to understand what I was saying. That moment though, where God took my heavy burden and turned it into a blessing? Oh, girl, do you see it yet? He is just waiting for us to ask! Take it to Him, all of it—everything you have and don't have—and wait for it. He might not give you exactly what you want, but I bet He'll give you more. And you know what else?

He is so here for it all.

Can you see it yet? The pattern of God's provision? God took something in my heart that would be menial to most people. A story of nothing more than a sweeper, but He turned it into a reminder of His faithfulness for His children. He is doing the same for you. He took the remnants of brokenness and reminded me that even when I was at my very lowest places, when my hands were far too heavy for me to even lift to the heavens in praise, only could I sit with my palms open saying, "Here I am, Lord, and I have nothing to give you. I have brokenness, a failed marriage. Scars from verbal abuse, emotional confusion, loneliness, all of the things that are terrible and ugly. That's all I have, but take it, take me, and show me that you still want me."

He did. If He can take the story of a sweeper and turn it into the promise of His provision then He can take your failures and struggles, your losses, angst, and betrayal and turn them in to things far greater than we can ever imagine.

It's our own humanity that separates us from the ability to recognize that only this sovereign Deity could want us with our conditional desires and love and still give us unconditional forgiveness and love right back. What a mighty God we serve. That story still gives me chills. It still serves as a reminder to my heart that even in the smallest portions of our story, God is working on our behalf. He is weaving together plans for our futures that would never dare insult us or belittle us. He is providing a way for us to have what we will need but not always when we think we need it. No; instead, when He *knows* we will need it. *I believe that He gives us these gifts and moments to remind us, "See, even the tiniest details of your life are important to me!"* Can you just imagine what He thinks about the big details? Oh, my goodness. I can just see Him up there working on all these plans and architectural designs for our lives that are no doubt grandeur.

His design for our lives is nothing short of that. He was the grand designer of this universe, and He is the grand designer of your life, girl. Like a puzzle with thousands of pieces all being laid together in accordance with one another. First, He picks up the pieces we see scattered on the floor. Next, He takes the rough edges and pieces them together, making sure a foundation is being set. Slowly starting.

Then, He works on the inside. Maybe the fuzzy pieces all get laid down together or organized into neat piles. No matter the rhythm of His divine artwork, you can be assured that each piece is placed into our unique puzzles just at the exact, right timing. I believe as the puzzle comes together, He smiles.

"See how beautiful this section over here is? See how I put those awkward pieces together to create a beautiful montage? Those rough edges that seemed confusing? They laid so nicely together and created a beautiful background for the soon-to-be finished product."

But that's a life's work. The finished product. We won't get to that ending until we meet our Maker. Until the day that all Christians should desire to hear, *"Well done good and faithful servant."* And then I hope that He will pull out my puzzle and say, "Let me show you how all of this worked! Remember this moment? Here's where it all came together. *Look* how beautiful you are!"

And that's just how all this works, sister. I could write to you many more stories about how God has shown up in my life. From the time I was a premature newborn and God spared my life, to being a teenager who grew up in a church where my grandfather was the pastor. Within those church walls we experienced scandal, betrayal, and brokenness both in family and as a church family long before these things were a trend. But how those moments shaped the people around me would forever impact and alter my life.

I would love to tell you how my nickname for my entire life has never been Mack, although I was named after my grandpa, and not Kenzie either. Instead, it was always Grace, simply because I have always been lanky and awkward enough to trip and stumble over myself. Sarcasm brought me that name and look how God wove it into my life's story. Remember that letter from my aunt? She called me Grace, but this time it was for my refining. Skip ahead to my college years when God told me I would become a teacher, if only ten years later for the fact that it would be the sole reason I obtained legal custody of my daughters. To experiencing brutal heartbreak in the hellfires of divorce, only allowing room for the refinement that can happen within.

But all of those stories are mine. Not yours…

Charge

*A*nd now, *dear girl, this is your time.*

God has allowed your trial and testing to pass before His throne. He has ordained this examining of your faith in this season of your life. I can assure you that this won't end overnight, and the tests may come at every twist and turn. Some days you will fight for sanity every minute and others it may come with ease.

Sister in Christ, take all that He has entrusted you with—His gift of salvation, His blessings, His faithfulness, His unconditional love—and plant them deep within the ashes of your wounded heart. Water them with His grace and the truths of His word daily. Saturate your heart with praises and cast down your desires in the battlefield of prayer. Lay down the shovel, and let God do the pruning. Then allow the Son to shine His warmth on you, and one day you will turn around and see a garden. You will look around and witness the beautiful fruits of the spirit that will emerge from the ashes and make their appearances as the Great Gardener of our lives completes a good work within you.

One day, you might share your story of hope with women just like me and you. Women who need so badly to know of the ultimate love that only One Man can truly give. And then, dear girl, then you will share your testimony of how you, too, became…

Grace under Fire.

The End

About the Author

Mackenzie is a thirty-something, remarried mother of two. She enjoys the finer things in life like volunteering at her children's school, reading C. S. Lewis, and drinking all the coffee. After walking through her own unanticipated and heartbreaking divorce, she made the choice to lay down her hurt and let God do the work. Through pen and paper, God has offered lesson after lesson of healing and hope that Mackenzie keenly desires to share with so many hurting women in our world today.

Her heart is most content when she is passionately writing to encourage other women. Mackenzie is a firm believer in the divine connection found within community. Her goal is to help women overcome pain from their past, find grace within their fire, and seek refinement through Jesus Christ.